Motorcycle Messengers
tales from the road by writers who ride

Edited by Jeremy Kroeker
Foreword by Ted Simon

Library and Archives Canada Cataloguing in Publication

Motorcycle Messengers: tales from the road by writers who ride / edited by Jeremy Kroeker

ISBN 978-0-9918250-1-1

Photos by Alfonse Palaima, motophotography.com
Cover by Scott Manktelow Design, ScottManktelow.com

Editor: Jeremy Kroeker
Copy Editor: Jennifer Groundwater

Printed and bound in Canada

Oscillator Press
670, 743 Railway Ave.
Canmore, Alberta
T1W 1P2 Canada

OscillatorPress.com

Books by Jeremy Kroeker

Motorcycle Therapy
Through Dust and Darkness

For Nevil Stow,
inventor of the garagarita
(part beverage, part experience).

Foreword

Ted Simon

I couldn't be more enthusiastic about a collection of stories by bikers. After all, the foundation that bears my name is dedicated to encouraging exactly this kind of thing—and yet I recognize that for many readers, there is something odd about the expectation that motorcyclists would produce literature. That was the main reason why Pirsig's book *Zen and the Art of Motorcycle Maintenance* created such a sensation. The juxtaposition of bikes and philosophy was bizarre enough to titillate ordinary readers (by "ordinary," I naturally mean non-riders) who would normally never touch a bike with a dipstick. Fortunately, the book was good enough to sustain their interest. Of course it was more—much more—about philosophy than biking, just as my own books are much more about travel than motorcycles. Indeed, most of the stories in this collection have more to do with the world around the rider than the machine he rides. So what is the justification for putting them all together in one volume?

It's not just a gimmick.

I maintain that people who use a motorcycle to travel have a sharper, truer view of everything around them. It's a necessity for survival. The need to be always alert, always ready to deal with some unexpected contingency, greatly enhances the perception or, as Dr. Johnson put it in a different context, it concentrates the mind wonderfully. What would be an inconvenient and expensive accident in a car can be fatal on a bike. Precisely because they are so vulnerable and dependent on their environment, riders are better equipped to cross over cultural divides.

Unlike their four-wheeled brethren who are protected and separated from the world in their steel cages, motorcyclists are visible human beings and, especially in remote areas where motorcycles are not so common, they engender curiosity and sympathy. Wise riders take advantage of this; they travel slowly, stop to ask for directions, to talk, to drink a cup of tea, to find out what's going on, and accept invitations. Generally, they have a much broader experience of the warmth and generosity that still, thank heavens, persist among people of all kinds everywhere. This is the message they carry with them, from host to host, from country to country, and eventually back home. There is abundant evidence of that in these stories.

Ted Simon
California, U.S.A.
2015

Stories

Doing the Congo 9
Lois Pryce

Alcohol Was a Factor 22
Ted Bishop

African Commuter 29
Mark Richardson

Chinese Hitchhiker 37
Carla King

Road Magic 46
Sam Manicom

Adventure Trio: The Great Divide or Bust! 57
Sandy Borden

Just One for the Road! 65
Paddy Tyson

The Sweet Science 71
Neil Peart

Riding in the Rain 78
Jeremy Kroeker

The Heart of Morocco 84
Issa Breibish

Motorcycle Safari 92
Dom Giles

The Great Question 99
Chris Becker

High on the Plateau 106
Carl Parker

The Cedars of God 114
Jeremy Kroeker

Missed a Date with the Sausage Creature 119
Andreas Schroeder

Ladakh and Zanskar 125
Geoff Hill

Five Bikes 136
Mark Richardson

Return to the Bay of Pigs 143
Christopher P. Baker

A Two-Wheeled Vision Quest 153
Nicole Espinosa

Robbers! Robbers! Robbers! 159
Jordan and Sandra Hasselmann

Nowhere to Go 170
Jeremy Kroeker

Iran 178
Geoff Hill

Living is Risky 196
Mark Richardson

No Politics for Lebanon's Hogs 212
Jeremy Kroeker

The Good Ship Chidambaram 215
Ted Simon

Young, Wild, and Riding Free 227
Natalie Ellis Barros

Afterword 234
Jeremy Kroeker

Acknowledgements 236

Doing the Congo

Lois Pryce

The following is an excerpt from the book Red Tape and White Knuckles, *published in the U.K. by Arrow, an imprint of Penguin Random House, and in the U.S.A. by Octane Press (OctanePress.com). Used with permission.*

The usual hoo-hah involving small men with big rubber stamps was particularly drawn-out and painful, requiring a constant stream of cash and an industrial scale of photocopying. By the end of it even Ricky, my self-appointed helper, was starting to look a bit stressed, and we lost his friend Kevin somewhere along the way when he got roughed up and thrown out of an office by an angry hulk of a man in a grey uniform. Eventually Ricky beckoned me to follow him aboard the ferry, and I rode up the rickety gangplank, clanking my way onto the boat. It was a rusting old iron heap that comprised no more than a covered deck and a few rows of seats for passengers. I parked my bike facing out towards Kinshasa and stared over the water, feeling more apprehensive than ever before on my journey.

There were plenty of men and women coming aboard, carrying enormous sacks of grain on their heads, several men who were already drunk at nine in the morning, and a surprisingly large number of cripples dragging themselves around on their withered limbs, or being pushed aboard in homemade Heath Robinson-style wheelchairs. I asked Ricky why there were so many of them, and he sneered distastefully.

"They are trouble, big trouble. They can travel cheap on the ferry, so they go back and forth, selling and buying between Brazzaville and Kinshasa; they sell cheaper than everyone else, and they smuggle things too. They are trouble, very aggressive when they are all together like that. You must not talk to them."

I watched them arranging themselves and their strange collection of wheelchairs and tricycles piled up with goods. Africa is probably the worst place in the world to be disabled, but they were getting on with it, survivors making something of their pitiful lives. But they all had the look that I now knew so well: the cold, empty eyes of the Congo.

A few able-bodied chancers were diving off the wharf into the brown swirling water and swimming round to the other side of the boat, where they clambered aboard to avoid paying for a ticket. One of them was even carrying a sack of rice while he carried out this manoeuvre, holding it on his head and swimming with his free arm.

A burst of shouting and banging drew my attention away to the top of the gangplank, where an elderly woman and one of the deckhands were in the midst of a fistfight. She punched him in the chest, then he shoved her up against a bulkhead. Her skull made a dull clanking sound as it came into contact with the rusty iron wall; fortunately she was wearing a large and elaborate headdress, which hopefully softened the blow. Not to be deterred, she came back at him with a right hook in the face, which he returned immediately. It was the Rumble in the Jungle for the twenty-first century: Ali and Foreman had nothing on these two as they continued to batter each other, sometimes rolling on the floor, but always coming up for more. It was turning into quite a commotion as more passengers boarded the ferry, pushing their way past the scrapping couple. In the end some of the heftier-looking males on board, including Ricky, steamed in and successfully pulled them apart.

"What was all that about?" I asked Ricky when the excitement had died down. The elderly woman was sitting alone, perched on a sack of rice, her face clouded with fury.

"Oh, nothing. She is his mother; they are always fighting," he explained with a shrug.

Ricky bid me farewell. He had other business to attend to, more scams and fixes to take care of, and, no doubt, more fights to break up.

"Good luck in Kinshasa," he said, shaking his head.

Now that Ricky had gone and the drama of the fight had subsided, attention was turned towards me and I was soon surrounded by a curious crowd. They formed a circle around me and the bike and stood there staring, except for one particular man who was steaming drunk and insisted on lurching towards me and draping his arm round my shoulders. Each time he did this I would hop round the other side of the bike, but he always followed, staggering and slurring after me, sending me skipping off back to the other side, until I was trotting non-stop around the bike with him in hot pursuit. It was straight out of *The Benny Hill Show*; the only thing missing was a novelty theme tune. This ridiculous carry-on continued for some time until one of the young men in the crowd hauled him away with a few choice words and a look of disgust. Drunks, the disabled, old women; there was no respect for these weak, lowly members of society in the Congo. It was survival of the fittest, quite literally the law of the jungle.

I thanked the man for coming to my rescue and this dialogue prompted a wave of questions from the crowd. As each one spoke, it encouraged the others and soon I was under siege from a non-stop interrogation. Where was my husband? Where was I from? Where was I going? And again and again: Where was my husband? I told various lies by way of response, but my inquisitors were quick to warn me that I shouldn't even be thinking of going to Kinshasa, repeating everyone's warning that it was "very dangerous for a woman alone." I made up a lie that my husband was waiting for me there, but they wanted to know why he wasn't with me, where he was exactly, where would we be staying? I was thinking on my feet and made up a fantastically elaborate story which they seemed to buy, but I still felt thoroughly unnerved and as the crowd swelled, moving in closer and the questions and warnings came thicker and faster, I felt distinctly panicky. Overcome with dizziness and nausea, I forced myself to breathe slowly and deeply and stay calm, but it was easier said than done. It seemed to me that by taking this ferry to Kinshasa, I was jumping out of the frying pan and into the blazing, fiery depths of Hades. When the boat cast off from the dock, my heart was thumping fast at the thought of what awaited me on the other side of the river.

The crowd continued to stare at me, but the questions subsided and mercifully everyone's attention was diverted to a scuffle on top of the roof where one of the ticketless chancers was hiding out. I had seen him swim round, climb aboard and then leg it up a pole on to the corrugated iron roof. But the deckhands had seen all the tricks before and it wasn't long before he was rumbled. There was burst of shouting above us before a lithe black body sailed past, landing like a bomb in the churned-up water. Whether he jumped or was pushed, I didn't know, but he broke into a fast front crawl and it looked highly likely that he would make it to Kinshasa before the rest of us.

The crossing of the river took half an hour. In some way I wished it would never end, that I could float indefinitely in limbo, that I would never have to make my nerve-wracking entry into this most awful of African nations. As we left Brazzaville behind and the hazy image of Kinshasa's tower blocks became steadily clearer, I became more and more fraught. Now I wished the boat would just hurry up and get on with it and spare me this slow and dreadful countdown.

I could see the chaos of Kinshasa port before we even touched the bank. As the boat edged in to moor, people were already jumping on from the quayside, making daredevil leaps across the water. The port officials were screaming orders, to no avail: everyone was yelling at each other and throwing their sacks of rice and bulging Chinese laundry bags on and off the boat. I sat on the bike and waited for the mayhem to subside before making a speedy run up the ramp. But I didn't get very far. My passage was quickly blocked by a mob of aggressive, shouting men who were grabbing hold of my arm, waving fake IDs in my face and yelling orders at me: *Show me your passport! Get over there! Where are you going? Stay there! Show me your papers!*

If they were attempting to intimidate me, they were succeeding, but I knew immediately that my usual tactic of smiling patiently and being extra-polite would have no currency in this situation, and I'd long since realized that damsel-in-distress mode doesn't work in this part of the world. Chivalry is a rare commodity in Africa, and the women are as tough as the guys; they have to be, considering their position in the pecking order, which is somewhere above the animals, but below the men. As I sat there on the bike with my engine running, slipping the clutch on the steep ramp, I knew there was only one way I was going to get out of this situation unscathed. It was time to dig out and dust off my hard-nosed side; if I didn't, I was likely to burst into tears, and that would be the worst thing I could do. I got the feeling that people had stopped crying in the Congo a long time ago.

It was a strange sensation to make a conscious decision to act like a seriously stroppy bitch, as there's not much call for this kind of activity in my regular day-to-day life, but it was reassuring to know that I could draw upon it in an emergency. I stayed sitting on the bike, made what I hoped was a don't-mess-with-me-face and started yelling at everyone, telling them where to stick their fake ID cards and to get the hell out of my way. I was almost laughing as I heard myself; I sounded quite ridiculous, but amazingly, it worked. The men made a feeble show of being threatening, but then slowly, one by one, they skulked off into the crowd, leaving me free to ride up the ramp and into the fenced-off yard where the real trouble would begin: dealing with the men with the genuine ID cards.

There were no signs suggesting where I should go; all the buildings were unmarked and equally shabby; and, to make matters more confusing, none of the men who claimed to be customs and immigration officials was wearing any kind of uniform. There was no way of telling them from the hordes of dodgy fixers that I had successfully banished at the quayside, and once again I found myself at the mercy of yet more shifty, steely-eyed men. To add to the fun, there was now the added delight of being mobbed by legions of money-changers waving wads of Congolese francs in my face.

Luckily I was taken in hand by a young chap by the name of Jean-Paul who I immediately liked, partly because he spoke English and partly because he was a bit chubby and showed the beginnings of a slight paunch under his too-tight T-shirt. There was something quite sweet about him, but I was forever wary about who to trust and once again had only my instinct on which to rely. But my instinct had been getting a good workout lately and it came up trumps again. Jean-Paul never left my side, guiding me over the hot coals of the D.R.C's entry formalities, most of which were conducted on the bonnet of a decrepit seventies Mercedes under a fierce midday sun.

Customs went pretty smoothly, aside from the unwanted attentions of a one-legged officer who called me into a vast, gloomy hangar on the pretext of examining my bike and made various lascivious suggestions, some of which involved me sitting on his stump. Mercifully, Jean-Paul came to the rescue and steered me back outside into the glaring sunlight, where a man from Immigration wanted to have a word with me.

Perched on the bonnet of the Mercedes, he appeared to be proofreading every page in my passport. He turned to me, his eyes hidden behind mirrored sunglasses for maximum intimidation, and I could see the reflection of my pale, anxious face staring back at me. It occurred to me that I couldn't be more out of place.

"So, where were you before you came here?" he said.

"I was in Brazzaville, in Congo."

"And before that?"

"Gabon."

"And before that?"

"Cameroon."

He said nothing, but flicked through the pages in silence, studying the dates of my visas and stamps to see if they matched my story.

"Let me see your vehicle papers," he demanded.

I fished them out of my luggage and he laid everything out on the bonnet, double-checking and cross-referencing every single date, right back to when I had entered Tunisia, before copying it all down into a book.

"But you say you come from England. Where did you go from England? Not to Tunisia, no?"

"I took a boat to France, and then another boat to Tunis."

"There is nothing in here of France!" He slammed my passport down on the bonnet triumphantly, and I realized how the car had become so dented.

"If you're English you don't get stamped in France; it's in the EU," I said, trying not to sound too much of a smartarse. I wanted to add "Duh!" at the end of my statement, but I feared it would not help my cause.

He obviously had no idea what I was talking about and continued picking through my papers, determined to find something—anything— untoward that would provide him with the evidence he needed to extract a big, juicy bribe. Meanwhile, sensing that cash would soon be changing hands, the vulture-like money-changers were circling again, but as Jean-Paul shooed one away, another would appear in his place. Oh, sweet, civilized Europe! I thought, with a sudden pang for its open borders, its temperate climate, and its single monetary policy.

Confounded by the European question, the immigration officer instead quibbled over smudged visa stamps, questioned the sloppy handwriting of the Nigerian officials, tested me to see if I could remember what dates I had entered and exited each country, and accused me of lying when I failed to recall each one correctly. Jean-Paul was hopping around, trying to reason with him on my behalf, but was blatantly ignored or barked at occasionally. The sun was blazing high in the sky now and even the broken-up tarmac beneath my feet was radiating heat, but our man from Immigration was immune to the fierce rays burning down on us, and continued to interrogate me as I perched on the car bonnet feeling distinctly weak and light-headed under the glare of the cruel Kinshasa sun and its equally cruel bureaucracy. How is it possible, I marvelled, that this amount of attention to detail is lavished on completely unnecessary red tape and bullshit while the rest of this country's affairs are in a state of complete meltdown?

The immigration officer didn't like it, but eventually he had to admit it: there was nothing he could get me on. My papers were whiter than white, except for my faked Cameroon exit date which had sailed past his supposedly eagle eyes. He slammed my documents down on the car bonnet and made an invisible nod that meant I was free to go. I smiled at him, enjoying my mini-victory; my spotless admin had triumphed over corruption! But my euphoria was short-lived, as it was now the turn of the policemen, and they wanted to see the contents of my luggage laid out on the ground.

Jean-Paul began a plea in my defense, but was banished to the sidelines as they picked over my belongings. The money-changers were still hovering, but they were blending into the crowd that had come to watch me unpack my kit. I recognized some of the faces: the one-legged customs man and a few of the guys who had questioned me on the ferry were there, as well as some of the disabled men in their hand-pedalled carts. With a quick glance, I approximated that my audience averaged about 1.75 legs per person.

"This is for me, yes, a gift for me?" said one of the officers, an older guy with a cunning, lined face. He was holding up a bottle of liquid soap.

"Er, yes, I s'pose so," I shrugged. If soap was all he was after, I had got away lightly.

"And this," said his younger sidekick, flicking through my French-English dictionary, "I like this, I learn English, yes?" he giggled.

"Yeah, sure, knock yourself out." If all went to plan, I would be in Angola in a couple of days and my French dictionary would be redundant. In fact, these guys were doing me a favour, lightening my load, just as long as they left me my Portuguese phrasebook.

"Why are you here in Kinshasa? Where are you going?" the older officer asked me with a hint of suspicion. "You are married, yes?" He seized my left hand and stared at my wedding ring. I was getting used to being grabbed by complete strangers, and I barely flinched.

"I'm meeting my husband. He's here in Kinshasa," I replied, rolling out the old line.

"But where is he? Why is he not with you?"

I started to launch into my elaborate cover story, but I couldn't remember the full details. To make matters worse, I was surrounded by various people to whom I had already told all sorts of lies, and with the overbearing heat and the pressure of the situation, I was becoming confused about what I had said to whom. Thankfully one of the guys from the ferry unknowingly came to my rescue.

"Her husband is at the embassy, the embassy for Great Britain," he shouted to the policeman. This was just the cue I needed.

"Er … yes, yes, he's at the embassy," I concurred.

"But why is he not with you?" The officer simply couldn't understand how this could be.

It was all coming back to me now, and my fabrications tripped off my tongue. Luckily, the finicky immigration officer was not present to challenge my quickly-rewritten history.

"We were travelling together, but when we were in Brazzaville, I had to go back to England, and while I was away, his visa ran out, so he came here. Then I flew back to Brazzaville and now I am catching up with him."

"So he came through here, through Kinshasa?" The policeman sounded suspicious.

"Er, yes."

"He is riding a motorcycle, like you?"

"Yes," I said, a little uncertainly. This was one nosey police officer.

"I have not seen an English man on a motorcycle here," he said, his eyes narrowing.

"Uh …" I tried to avoid his stare, not knowing what to say. But I was saved by his colleague piping up.

"Yes, yes! I see him, he is with a friend, yes?" he said, turning to me. "Two motorcycles, big motorcycles, one is red, yes? They are here two weeks ago!"

What on earth was he on about? Then the realization dawned on me; he was talking about the two motorcyclists from Portsmouth that I had heard about. They were ahead of me by about two weeks and unbeknownst to them, they had saved my bacon in a most miraculous fashion.

"Yes, yes, that was him!" I agreed a little too eagerly.

The policemen both nodded, reassured and I suppressed a roar of laughter at this coincidental stroke of good fortune.

"But why do you go back to England without him?" asked the older officer.

"Well," I said, putting on a sad face and lowering my voice, "my grandmother died over Christmas so I had to go back home for her funeral."

It worked every time. A murmur of sympathy passed through the crowd and this band of cruel, hard men poured out their condolences. One thing they knew about in this country was death.

"Ah, I am very sorry. Very sorry about your grandmother," said the older policeman, now gripping both of my hands.

I nodded and thanked them for their kindness, trying to look suitably grief-stricken. I didn't feel too guilty, as both my grandmothers had been dead for years, and I'm sure they wouldn't have objected to me misusing their identities to help me out of a hole such as this.

Despite that burst of compassion, the dead grandmother was soon forgotten, and nothing would stop the police getting on with the business in hand. The men continued to rifle through the rest of my clobber, choosing a few more "gifts"—a cigarette lighter and a marker pen—but I didn't mind too much; I was just relieved they possessed such humble tastes. Looking pleased with their haul, they wandered off, examining their prizes, leaving me to pack up and go. The Democratic Republic of the Congo was mine for the taking.

Lois Pryce is a British travel author, journalist and broadcaster. She is also co-founder of the Adventure Travel Film Festival.

In 2003 Lois left her job at the BBC in London to ride twenty thousand miles from Alaska to the tip of South America on a small dirt bike. Her book about this trip, Lois on the Loose, *has been published throughout the world.*

In 2006 she rode the length of Africa, taking in the Sahara, the Congo and Angola, which resulted in her book, Red Tape and White Knuckles.

In 2013/14, intrigued by the negative image of Iran and its stormy relationship with her homeland, she made two solo motorcycle tours of the Islamic Republic—and discovered a misunderstood country full of warmth and kindness. This is the subject of her next book.

With her husband, adventure filmmaker Austin Vince, she is founder/curator of the Adventure Travel Film Festival, which occurs annually in the UK and Australia.

Web: LoisOnTheLoose.com

Alcohol Was a Factor

Ted Bishop

It was a hard ride down to Oregon: the wind in the Crowsnest Pass bobbled my head back and forth like a guy throwing pizza dough hand to hand, and by the time I got to Coeur d'Alene I had grooves in my lower butt cheeks from the buckles on the saddlebag straps—a Ducati Monster doesn't have much cargo space. At the visitor centre, I thought I was getting an electric shock from the counter, but it was just the tingling from hours of gripping the handlebars. As I did at some point on every motorcycle tour, I wondered why I was doing this.

I was working on a book called *The Social Life of Ink* and when I learned about a man in Utah who made Gutenberg-replica printing presses, I had to go see him. The printer, Steve Pratt, refused email and avoided the phone. This seemed like a good excuse to extend a ride: I was going to the Tynda motorcycle rally anyway and thought, Easy: I'll bop down to Eugene, Oregon, nip across to Utah, and swing home to Edmonton. A big triangle with a flat base. Somehow I had failed to notice that the Pratt ranch was far south of Eugene, and that I would be crossing the great Nevada desert.

But, of course, the only way I get anywhere interesting is through willful self-delusion—an essential character trait for both motorcyclists and writers. If you allowed yourself to think realistically about either enterprise, you would never start.

The best stretch came when I dropped down through eastern Oregon and found route 395, a glorious 117-mile road that climbs and winds and falls through pine forests from Pendleton to Mt. Vernon. I fetched up, tired but happy, at the El Teulito restaurant in a town called John Day, with a Negra Modelo, chips, salsa, and a chicken fajita. The sagging Naugahyde seats of the booth put the table at my chest. (After years of wondering, I looked up Naugahyde on my Oxford English Dictionary phone app. No Naugas had been killed in the making of this booth. Naugahyde is "the proprietary name for a material used in upholstery, consisting of a fabric base coated with a layer of rubber or vinyl resin and finished with a leather-like grain;" the stuff comes from Naugatuck, a town in Connecticut where rubber is manufactured).

The Naugahyde wasn't the only thing that was worn out. When I left the motorcycle rally, I nicked the upper-right corner of California, riding south from Klamath Falls through the Medoc National Forest to Reno, Nevada. A long day on a tight bike, and as I steered it into the Nugget casino, shoulders knotted, hands clenched, legs in a tight zed, I thought I might just fall over. The Ducati and I weren't as young as we once were. I was coming up on 60 (years, not miles per hour) and knew this was my last tour on the Monster.

The next day, rain started to fall, and for the first time ever the bike began to buck and stumble. Water in the fuel line? The engine stalled and caught with each downshift, making the rear tire grab and slip on the wet pavement. The desert was cold, and I'd taken on too much territory. I coughed into Ely and pulled up in front of the Hotel Nevada.

There were two characters out front, protected from the rain by the sign that jutted out over them: FRESHHOME MADEPIZZA 24HRS. It looked like the lone bench was their home. The stocky guy with a buzz cut sat. The other guy—tall and skinny, in a plaid shirt, baseball cap, and glasses—leaned forward like a prof at a non-existent lectern, bony finger extended, lecturing his colleague.

Maybe that's how I'd wind up. As an English prof, I'd spent my life immersed in ink and now I'd become obsessed with the stuff. "A substance so common we never really see it!" I'd say, rattling on about ballpoint pen inventor Lazlo Biro and capillary action. People were starting to back away from me at dinner parties.

I'd planned to toss off a slim volume in a year; now I was three years into it and the book was spreading like a blob. If I'd known the project would take me another five years—and take me to China, Uzbekistan, and the edge of Tibet—I'd have bagged it right then and joined the guys on the bench.

I checked in (10% discount for bikers and a free margarita) and read the pamphlet: built in 1929, the Hotel Nevada was for years the highest building in the state. The four-storey-high mural of a six-gun-toting burro flipping flapjacks over a fire was famous, and Jimmy Stewart and Mickey Rooney had stayed here. Swell, but my cramped room with its feeble lamp and single kitchen chair hadn't been upgraded since Jimmy Stewart's famous stutter left the screen.

At the Chinese restaurant across the street, I ordered hot-and-sour soup and my spoon clattered against the little bowl. I was still chilled through. I'd hoped my bike would dry out, but the clouds settled in and the rain fell without respite. Back at the room, I sat on a hard kitchen chair wedged between the bed and the wall, and wrote by the light of the neon sign outside. I was on Route 50, America's Loneliest Highway.

In the morning, the bike would not start. The battery was strong, and the engine cranked and cranked, but would not catch. Ka-chuhh, Ka-chuhh. It sounded like a washing machine in the rinse cycle.

"Dude, sounds like you got water in the fuel line. You can get a bottle of alcohol for ninety-nine cents at the drugstore across the street."

The skinny guy I'd seen sitting in front of the hotel yesterday had appeared at my side. He looked like fifty miles of bad road and had that musty homeless smell. Without asking, he bent down and pulled off my spark plug lead.

"It's wet in there, dude."

I asked if there was an auto parts store. He directed me up the street, and I bought a bottle of starter fluid to spray into the carbs. "How much did you pay for that? Six bucks?! That alcohol, ninety-nine cents, would work just as well." He looked like he would know.

I phoned the local motorcycle mechanic, André, who came in five minutes. We took off the air filter, and sprayed the fluid into the carbs. I knew this was not good for the engine. When I lived in Kingston, I had an old 356 Porsche that sucked the Ontario humidity into its carbs, and in the wet fall I would get flames out the top of the motor when I used this stuff. Still, it dried things out.

The engine snapped and popped, and almost-but-not-quite caught. André looked concerned, solicitous. "Here's what I'd like to do. I'd like to take your bike into my shop where I can have a proper look at it. Not out here in a parking lot." What to do? He was oily and a titch too eager. But I said okay.

"Dude," said Dave (I'd learned his name) when André had gone, "Don't do this. All these small towns are hurting. Since the recession hit there's nothing going on. If he gets your bike in his shop it's going to be all day and at least a couple hundred bucks. I'm telling you, ninety-nine cents at the drugstore …"

He was right. Those had been dollar signs in André's helpful eyes.

I ran across the street, bought a bottle of rubbing alcohol ($1.69, not 99¢—maybe Dave got a special rate) and poured half into the gas tank.

Ka-chook, ka-chook, ka-chook—sounded like hiccups—ka-chook-BAM ka-chookBAM—it was catching—chookBAM! chookBAM! BAM-BAM-BAM!

I didn't know if the bike was running or blowing up. It roared and snapped and spat black smoke through the pipes and out the top of the engine.

"Why is it doing that?" I shouted to Dave.

"Because the air filter isn't on yet."

Right. Soon the explosions turned to normal combustion as the water in the line cleared, and the engine settled into a silky idle.

"Best I've heard it in years," I said to Dave.

I buckled my panniers on quickly before André could return with his trailer. I thought of all those zombie movies where bad things happen in small towns. When I was almost loaded Dave said, "Since I helped and all, d'you think you could spare a fiver? Or a ten …?"

"Nope," I said and he backed away. "I'm giving you twenty. You saved me money, and a lot of time, and somebody messing around with my engine. Thanks!" I gave him the money, cinched my tank bag, and was going to wave a final goodbye, but he was already heading back toward his bench.

Out in the desert I was alone for long stretches, and I wondered if my great-uncle Jeremiah had travelled that way. In 1852, age twenty-seven, he had taken the stagecoach from Ontario out to Sacramento, where instead of panning for gold in the California gold rush he bought into the *Sacramento Bee* newspaper, taking notes as a reporter in the morning and setting type in the afternoon. A friend said, "I guess you come by your interest in ink honestly."

His trip would have taken three jostling weeks. You perched on a bench seat, your knees dovetailed with the other passengers if you were in the rear-facing front row, swaying with only a leather strap for backrest if you were in the middle row, forced to get out and push up the hills or through mud holes.

You were asked not to drink but to share the bottle if you did, not to spit tobacco into the wind, not to cuss in front of ladies, not to snore on your neighbour's shoulder, not to hog the buffalo robes or shoot your guns out the window (it spooked the horses). Jeremiah's ride made my discomforts on a motorcycle look mild.

The rain had passed, leaving beautiful, washed-green sage and ridges soaked to a deep burnt sienna. High passes, big sky, and not the place for a breakdown. The Duc ran flawlessly but I still had the bottle of alcohol in my pocket, just like Dave, just in case.

Ted Bishop's book The Social Life of Ink: Culture, Wonder, and our Relationship with the Written Word *was published by Penguin-Random House Canada in 2014. Ted is also the author of* Riding with Rilke: Reflections on Motorcycles and Books.

Web: TedBishop.com

African Commuter

Mark Richardson

It was a Bajaj 100, and it sat with a bunch of other Bajajs in the back yard of the Kigali compound. The head courier looked at me and shrugged.

"Sure," he said, "You can take this one if you can fix it. Go right ahead."

I chose this one because it looked the least decrepit, but it still looked decrepit. The chain was hanging as loose as an old breast, and there was a thick film of rust on the muffler, handlebars and most everywhere there was metal. But it didn't look broken, and I set to with a wire brush and some oil and worked for the morning to clean it up.

The head courier thought me strange, as did all the other couriers. I was a Western manager for the aid agency he worked for, and there was a Toyota Land Cruiser available to me, with a driver. Yet I'd asked about the motorcycles and was even now dripping oil on the drive chain and forcing lubricant into the clutch and brake cables, in the shade of a tree out in the back yard. It made no sense.

In fact, the little bike didn't look too bad when I finished. It looked beaten-up, sure, as it certainly had been while running around through the honking traffic of Kigali, the capital of Rwanda, and perhaps out into the hills of the countryside. It hadn't been anywhere for quite a while, though. This was 1996 and the aid agency was still regrouping and reorganizing after the horrors of the recent genocide.

I was there as an "information officer," which meant I had to write regular reports about what was happening in the country that would be sent back to the agency's offices in North America and Europe, and I also had to help out any journalists who were still around, looking for stories. We all knew the biggest story was about to break: the refugees in the huge camps that neighboured Rwanda, in Tanzania and Zaire, were about to return home. I was on site and on top of it. That's why I'd been given a Land Cruiser to get around, to travel across the country and monitor the movement of hundreds of thousands of people.

But there was no reason why I shouldn't have some fun and ride a motorcycle instead, and I made this point to the Country Director when I requested a bike from the defunct courier fleet. Actually, I made the point that he could use the Land Cruiser for somebody else—himself, perhaps—and there was no need to tie up a driver for me. Most drivers were uneducated, with questionable licenses, anyway, and most Westerners preferred to sit them in the back and do the driving themselves.

So I fixed up the Bajaj 100 as best I could and then proudly showed it to the couriers. They admired the tightness of the chain, and nodded enthusiastically when I showed them how easily the levers pulled the cables. They stood back when I sat astride the bike and kicked its engine to life, and they watched politely as I roared up the road, the revs rising higher and higher. And higher. And higher.

I rode back more slowly. "It won't shift out of first," I said. "It must be a problem with the clutch." I parked the bike and squinted at everything that could be squinted at, but all seemed fine. I worked the cable and poked at things, then got back on the bike and rode it back up the road. Again, the couriers watched politely and listened to the little engine scream against its red line, and again, they watched me return, and they looked sad.

"I guess it's the transmission," I shrugged. "I should choose another bike."

A courier stepped forward. "May I try?" he asked, and I waved him toward the bike. He sat on it, kicked the kickstarter, listened to the engine, then set off up the road. I heard the motor's pitch rise and fall with each confident gear change, all the way to fourth. Then he turned around at the end of the road, put the bike into second and cruised gently back.

"I think, perhaps, you were using the pedal the opposite way," he told me with absolute courtesy, and of course he was right. The Bajaj was made in India and so its left pedal worked the rear brake and its right worked the gears. I already knew this, but even then, it was opposite to anything I'd ridden before: the gears were one push up, three pushes down. The courier had seen me jabbing the wrong way at the pedal when I wanted to shift into second, but had been too polite to mention it.

* * *

It took a week or so to get used to the opposite gearing, but I didn't let that stop me exploring the city and the local farmland. Rwanda was a very safe country at this time, partly due to a massive local military presence and partly due to the huge influx of foreign aid money that was rebuilding the infrastructure.

It was still a poor country, though, and life could be rough. For me personally, it was a challenge to work because I'd developed a blood clot in my right leg. There were no drugs to deal with the clot in Kigali, except

Aspirin, so a Belgian doctor bound up my leg very tight and told me to keep it elevated whenever possible. I did this, but I didn't want to return to Canada for treatment, so I just soldiered on with a bandaged leg. In truth, I had no idea just how potentially dangerous a blood clot could be, so I figured I'd deal with it once the refugees returned home.

In the meantime, I had to go visit the camps in Tanzania, which we expected to be the first to empty. The Country Director asked again if I wanted the Land Cruiser for the journey, about 200 kilometres that would take around four hours, but I saw no reason why I shouldn't ride the Bajaj and he was pleased to be able to keep the big SUV for others. Besides, I'd found a set of crash bars and could rest my leg up on them while riding.

I set off on this first big trip with a jerry can of gas strapped to the backrest and a litre of two-stroke oil strapped to the jerry can. I wore my rucksack, which rested on the passenger seat, and a helmet that would be rejected by your average kids' kart track. And I was happy. The bike ran well and the country was beautiful. Every hill was terraced and filled with fertile fields, a running tapestry of colour. It was a great ride, right up until the bike began to choke and slow down, coughing its way forward with hiccups of blue smoke from the tail pipe.

The problem was obvious: the spark plug was fouled, probably by crappy gas and poor carburetor adjustment. I was near a village—everywhere in Rwanda is near a village—and I limped to a halt near a mud-hut store, underneath a shade tree. Immediately, curious people walking who knows where paused to look and children gathered to giggle at the stranded *muzungu*.

I don't remember now if I already had a spark plug wrench or had to borrow one from somewhere in the village, but I do remember the oily blue and black tip of the spark plug once it was removed, and the heat of the metal as I wiped the plug on a rag. I also remember a young man approaching, as I laboured away, to offer me some tea, which I declined. The water could be suspect, and my Western resilience was no match for a stomach born and bred in the region. But when I'd finished and the plug was clean again, somebody else came up to sell me a cake and I took it gratefully. It was a good time for a break, after all—about halfway to the border. The young man offered me tea a second time, but I declined again and set off on my way.

When I reached Tanzania, the bike was running a little rough and so I found a wire brush and cleaned the plug a second time. I may have had a wrench already, but if I didn't, I bought one from a supplier and kept it in my pocket. I stayed a day and then started my return trip to Kigali. Once again, the bike began to cough near the same halfway point and I pulled over under the same tree and set about cleaning the plug. It would be quick work now, just a few minutes, but I burned my hands on the ticking metal, so I sat back to wait while the engine cooled.

"Would you like some chai?" I looked up and it was the young man from before, offering a china cup of chai tea already made. He looked so concerned—and so kind—that I accepted this time and sipped at the tea while the two of us talked about motorcycles for a while. He told me he had a bike himself, but it wasn't as good as mine. It was a step-through Honda. I told him that that was my first bike, and we both smiled happily as I enjoyed the tea and let the Bajaj cool a little in the shade. Another cake was offered and I was told it was a gift, but I insisted on paying the little boy who brought it and everyone seemed happy. I think I paid 10 times the local rate. Then after maybe half an hour of gentle conversation, I removed the plug, brushed and wiped it clean, topped up the gas tank and returned to Kigali.

I made that trip several times in the next few weeks, each time stopping at the same point, under the same shade tree, to clean the spark plug and enjoy some tea and pay too much money to a little boy for a cake. They knew me as the guy who liked to cruise on his bike with his right leg up on the crash bar or sometimes even up on the handlebar itself; I never admitted that underneath my long pants, the leg was bound like a cast. They found me entertaining and some people would wave at me on the road when I passed, though I was never sure if they knew me or were just being polite. The bike started to run better with careful maintenance and after a while, it really didn't need to have its plug cleaned so often, but I stopped to do it anyway. It was a chance for a break on the road to or from the border, and it was a chance to talk about motorcycles with people who thought a Bajaj 100 was something to be appreciated, something valuable.

One day, while visiting Tanzania, I was set to leave the next morning but woke at dawn to realize the camp had emptied. Tens of thousands of people had moved out in the night and slipped back over the border into Rwanda, to try to resume their lives as if nothing had happened. The camp was a shell of vacant stick huts and I limped door to door all day to make sure nobody had been left behind. Nobody had. The camp was abandoned, every one of the thousands of huts deserted.

I rode to Kigali the next day with my handwritten report in my back pocket. I needed to hurry back, to fax the pages to Europe and North America. The bike sang on the road, clean and responsive. After an hour or two, I came to the place where I would have cleaned the plug. I slowed down but didn't stop, and waved at the people there who waved back, then lifted their heads higher when they recognized me.

I thought of the tea. I thought of the cake. I thought of the gentle conversation that began to seem more important than any faxed report. Before I reached the curve in the road at the edge of the village, I slowed and turned and came back to park under the tree.

The report could wait for a little while. A young man offered me tea and a small boy offered me cake; I insisted on paying for it with a larger note than usual, which he accepted with bright eyes. The Bajaj 100 ticked away in the heat for a while as several of us talked about motorcycles. I told the story of pressing the gear pedal the wrong way and everybody laughed, and I showed them the bandages under my jeans and everyone looked concerned. "You must go home now, to fix yourself," somebody said and all agreed.

I didn't clean the plug that time—it didn't need it. I shook everyone's hand and swung my bad leg over the seat and started the bike, then pushed down on the pedal to put it into second gear. As I rode away from the village, I pushed twice more to find fourth gear before lifting my leg onto the crash bar to rest for the second half of the journey. In the mirror, I watched my friends waving goodbye under the shade tree until the road curved and they disappeared from view, and then I rode back to Kigali to fix myself.

Mark Richardson is an automotive writer who lives near Toronto and who loves a good road trip. He is the author of Zen and Now: On the Trail of Robert Pirsig and the Art of Motorcycle Maintenance, *for which he rode his old motorcycle across the United States to California. In 2012, he drove a new Chevy Camaro convertible along the entire 7,600-kilometre length of the Trans-Canada Highway and the journey became his second book,* Canada's Road: A Journey on the Trans-Canada Highway from St. John's to Victoria.

Web: ZenAndNow.org
Twitter: @WheelsMark

Chinese Hitchhiker

Carla King

At sunset I come upon a sign that tells me I am still 70 kilometres from Yinchuan, China, which is much farther than the map had indicated. Also, I am lost in the confused jumble of a new-looking town called Shizuishan, in a cul-de-sac near a cluster of apartment buildings. The main highway ended in a chaotic mix of streets and alleyways—no street larger than another, no sign indicating the way to Yinchuan … only shops and markets and pigs rummaging through piles of garbage.

Normally I would follow a blue truck—all the trucks in China are painted the same flat medium-blue colour—through the town to the highway, but it's dinnertime and the trucks are all parked in front of the restaurants. So I choose roads at random, roads that initially lead west toward the sunset, but that always veer north or south or even back eastwards. A low-grade panic sets in. I want out of this town, but I might not have time before nightfall and so I pull over to ask about *bing guan* and *lu guan* (inns), but people just shake their head no.

My very limited Beijing-accented Mandarin is not well understood by people in this region and, since they've had no contact with foreigners, they are too taken aback to comprehend me.

Soon I'm lost in a maze of factory complexes and apartment buildings, all brand-new. There is only one person on the street, a young man, and I pull over to ask the way to Yinchuan. He understands what I want, but his answer is so complex I can't follow. Finally, he jumps on the back of the Chang Jiang, as the sidecar is full of my luggage and a few spare parts, including an entire right side of the boxer twin, a piston and rings, just in case they bust again. The bike is 800 pounds of World War II engineering created by the Germans and used during the war by messengers travelling across bombed fields. Before the war, Hitler traded the entire factory to Stalin in exchange for natural resources like iron ore. It's assumed that somehow the Chinese got hold of a couple and reverse engineered them. So the machine is still made in the Ural mountains of Russia and was manufactured in a village by the Yangtze (Chang Jiang) river in China, now defunct. The military occasionally drags them out of warehouses to sell, and my Beijing-based friend Jim snaps them up for his friends. I imagine the original German machine was fairly reliable, made with quality metals and parts, but the Chinese versions are casually slapped together with inferior materials and so they clank and rattle apart easily. Luckily, the beasts are simply made and easy to fix. My mornings are spent in an hour-long inspection with liberal doses of Loctite and duct tape before I hit the road, and even then it can be dicey.

We ride around the factory and, with some alarm, I see we're headed straight toward a nuclear power plant. He says "Stop," and hops off. Apparently the road to Yinchuan is on the other side of the complex. Just ride around.

Before I can put the bike into first, two young men on a scooter pull up and block me, talking in urgent voices saying, "Yinchuan," over and over.

Am I going that way? It is a three-hour drive, they tell me. There is no hotel in this town. One of them will guide me to Yinchuan. No money. Go to Yinchuan now. Thank you.

I quickly make a decision: Okay, I'll take the guy with me. I'm not going to sleep outdoors next to a nuclear power plant. And even though I'll be riding in the dark, riding with a local is better than going alone. And besides, what am I here for—to play it safe?

"Okay, get on," I say.

Yes! Good! But he must stop by his apartment to get a couple of things. He points to the factory apartment complex, a collection of white buildings six storeys tall.

I hesitate. "No bad guy," he says, in English. "No bang bang pow pow," and then some babble, I think about a truck in Yinchuan.

So I drive him to his apartment complex and hurry with him upstairs. He is agile and quick. I am loaded down with fatigue … and by my leather jacket, boots, and helmet.

He runs out of sight ahead of me on the stairs, then runs back down to encourage me on, like a dog impatient for its master to follow. He lives on the top floor. There's a pile of bricks lying on the staircase and my paranoid side notes them as a potential weapons. Yes, in a pinch, I could bonk him on the head with one. I might need to … his manner has become manic.

I point to "hurry," and "trouble," in the phrasebook; he gives me a thumbs-up at "hurry" and thumbs-down at "trouble." He finds "friend," and "guide," and "no money," to make me feel better. I must be driving him crazy.

I'm surprised to find that the apartment is similar to a small two-bedroom apartment in the U.S. I stand in the living room as he runs around digging through drawers. He shows me his truck driver's card, holding it up to his face and pointing at the photo. He tells me to sit on the couch. Seconds later, he pushes a pair of black leather gloves into my hands and shows me their fur linings. Then he throws a pair of red cotton gloves, two tins of Tiger Balm, and some perfume onto the growing pile in my lap. The perfume smells vile, like mint and turpentine, but I smile and say thank you. My paranoia disappears into amusement and curiosity.

He rummages through more drawers, taking out a plastic model of a drag race car and running it through the air inches from my face, making a sound that must be the Chinese version of "vroom-vroom." Then he opens the door to the bedroom, which glows red because of the red lace curtains on the windows. He rifles through more drawers, runs to the kitchen to fill my tea jar with hot water, then dashes back into another room.

While he is busy, I walk around. The apartment is very nice, on the top floor, with a view of the factory and countryside beyond. It's neatly furnished, and it's got the first flush toilet I've seen in a month. On the wall is a wedding photo of him and his wife looking very young and sweet. He's wearing a tuxedo jacket and she a traditional Chinese red wedding dress, with lace overlaying the silk. For some reason, the photo calms me.

The phone rings. He has a hasty conversation. I get up to use the flush toilet. Actually I don't have to pee, but it's been so long since I've used an actual sit-down flush toilet that I think I must do it. It is a very pleasurable experience to pee with nobody watching, without having to duck into a ditch, farmers gawking, truckers driving by. The clean, cold porcelain is a joy. The warm water coming from the faucet in the sink almost magic, a towel for drying hands miraculously luxurious.

When I emerge, the man shoves my helmet and gloves, and the two other pairs of gloves, and the balm, and the perfume, into my hands. He shouts, "LET'S GO!" He literally runs in circles around me as I stand still, astounded.

"LET'S GO!"

We are off, down the stairs and getting on the bike just as his wife arrives. She must be at least eight months pregnant and seems astonished, gaping at me in disbelief. He talks and talks, and she looks from him to me and back again, unable to speak.

"SORRY!" he shouts to me. "LET'S GO!"

As I start the bike another woman cycles up and stops beside his wife. They stand there, staring. I feel bad that I can't reassure her, but it comforts me that somebody has seen us go, that someone knows who I'm with and where I'm going. They are definitely not happy, but the young man says goodbye and jumps on the back seat. He weighs maybe 100 pounds, maybe 90—not much more than the extra cylinder I have in the sidecar.

Again, he shouts "LET'S GO!" I shrug apologetically to the two women and jam the bike into reverse with the foot lever, turn, and follow his finger to the road.

The sun has set but there is still a little light. It is colder than I had thought it might get here in springtime, and I can feel the guy shaking behind me, clad only in his thin windbreaker. His hand trembles when he points the way. His hand moves in crisp jerks in front of my face, right or left or straight ahead.

My mind races. What is going to happen in Yinchuan? Does he have a family emergency? A job? Is he late for court? And then I get it. Truck, nervousness, shakes … drugs? He is running around like a maniac because he's a speed-freak trucker.

His truck is in Yinchuan for some reason and it shouldn't be. He took it there and will be in trouble if his boss knows. He had talked his friend into taking him on his scooter, but then they saw me.

"OohWHAAAH!" he yells in my ear when it looks like I may go straight instead of left.

"OohWHAAAH!" he yells when I move too far into the middle of the road.

"OohWHAAAH!" he yells when a truck jumps onto the highway ahead of us.

He reaches over my shoulder and points frantically at the ignition button, distracting me at exactly the wrong moment. A truck is passing in my lane dead ahead, I'm passing two bicyclists who are riding astride, a taxi is hot on my back bumper and beeping like crazy at me, and this guy is jabbing at my ignition button.

Why are you pushing the ignition? I want to ask, but I can't possibly. Then it dawns on me that he thinks it's the horn. To test the theory I beep the horn, which is on the other side.

"YYYYEEEESSS!" he yells in glee. "YYYYEEEESSS!"

It is now night and pitch-black. I am freezing, in spite of the fact that I'm wearing four shirts, a leather jacket, a wool scarf, a helmet and a rain suit. He is wearing slacks, a white shirt, a dinner jacket and a windbreaker. It becomes so dark that even the drivers who drive without their lights on turn on their lights—and that's when they start their sadistic little headlight-game power-trip.

I have no idea why they're flashing their high beams at me. I have the lows on, they flash their brights. I flash my brights, they blast me with their brights. They leave the lows on, and when they get ten feet away they turn on their high beams to blind me. All this while I'm trying to miss potholes, pass tractors and motorcycles and bicycles, and deal with Mr. "OohWHAAAH!" on my back seat.

Why can't they just put their dims on when they see an oncoming vehicle? It seems a simple rule, but it doesn't work here. I experiment. Dims on when I see them coming. Nope. They bright me. I bright back. They dim and bright back again. Okay. Brights on until they flash. But then if that happens they seem to get pissed off and bright me ten feet from touchdown. Too late to bright them back. Okay, so wait until we're about in irritation proximity, then dim. Seems to work best, but I still get blinded. "JERKS!" I yell.

"OohWHAAAH! I'M SORRY!" from the back seat. Oh yeah. He's a trucker. Getting a little taste of his own medicine, he is. Ha! So there.

Two hours later my left thumb is sore from hitting the bright-dim switch and the horn. Sometimes the switch gets momentarily stuck between settings and everything goes black. When that happens, there's an "OohWHAAAH!" followed by a hysterical laugh in my right ear.

We ride. The cold air creeps in through gaps in my clothes and I suppress a shiver, which has as much to do with the situation as with the cold. I didn't like the way he treated his wife, but then in China there is no public display of affection between husband and wife … none at all. And I feel sorry because she's pregnant and he's on drugs and off with a foreigner.

Two hours into it and he's still giving me directions on how to miss potholes and pass tractors. "I think I've come far enough through this crazy country without your help, thank you," I yell through my helmet and the wind, and he says, "YESSSS!" in delight. I begin to dislike him intensely, but then he starts the massage … a little chop-chop on the back, a little squeeze-squeeze on the shoulders. Some pieces of song that might be in English, another "OohWHAAAH!"

We're eighteen kilometres from Yinchuan but I have to stop and walk around for a few minutes. He lights a cigarette and starts babbling about this and that, (boshe, fellali, new yok) smokes, shakes his head, paces, and occasionally shouts in glee, "YINCHUAN – ONE – EIGHT – YES!"

We arrive in Yinchuan at eleven o'clock and my trucker helps me find a businessmen's hotel. He helps me get the motorcycle safely parked, locked, and covered. He runs ahead of me to open the door and helps me fill out the check-in form, translating for a very confused reception clerk. Then he brings my bags to my room, barks at the floor girl, washes his face, makes sure I have hot water in the thermos, tells me his name, which I can't understand, leaves, returns, asks me the time, turns on the television, and then leaves again.

I stand in front of the door, still wearing my layers of clothes and jacket, holding my helmet in one hand and the fleece-lined gloves he gave me in the other, waiting for him to remember one more thing and come back. But I never see him again.

Carla King's motorcycle misadventures began at age 14 in rural North Carolina when she identified the broken-down Honda Enduro in the barn as her escape vehicle. Her dad told her, "If you can fix it, you can ride it," unaware that he was setting her up for a career in adventure travel. She started with day-long jaunts through tobacco fields and creeks and—when the family moved to California—the coast and the mountains throughout the state. A six-week solo journey through France in the '80s led to months-long sojourns in Europe, China, Africa and India. In the mid-'90s Carla combined her love of travel, technology, mechanics, writing, and publishing to create the first real-time online travelogue (now called blogs), and began publishing her work and helping others self-publish.

Web: CarlaKing.com

Road Magic

Sam Manicom

The following story is an adaptation from the book Into Africa.

Conventional wisdom holds that only an experienced motorcyclist will
have the skills to be able to set off into any unknown, let alone Africa. I
now know that's not the case. I'd only been riding a bike for three months
when I nervously arrived on the shores of this amazing continent; my
mind was full of what-ifs. I countered my inexperience on a bike by planning to take it slowly, and knew that if there was an ounce of common
sense in me then I'd inevitably need to draw on every bit of it. Things
would go wrong, but I was sure that, in the end, respect towards everyone I met and luck would go a very long way. One I was in charge of, the
other …

What I hadn't taken into account was that once the ride had started
I'd be far too busy to be worrying. What was going to happen, was going
to happen.

One of the things that I love about travelling long distances is that you
really don't know what is going to crop up. I rather like that. I'd made it
across Europe and Egypt and was heading across the magic that is the Sudan. I'd been pinching myself a lot. This was me, riding a bike in Sudan!

I'd linked up with a couple of other riders. Mike and Sally were two-up on an old BMW bike and life was pretty darned good.

By seven-thirty in the morning, we were on the road out of the capital city of Khartoum and heading east. We reached the outskirts and fuelled the bikes before following perfect asphalt across the sunbaked countryside. For as far as I could see, the land was beige and the sky a clear blue. We were very glad to be free of the city; we had open road at last. The calm night air and heavy desert dew had settled the dust and the ground had yet to get so hot that the sky would be distorted by shimmering waves of heat. But the black surface of the road was a different story. Heat pounded up at us from it. The dry slipstream sucked moisture away from any bits of exposed skin and by 10:30 am it was 45 degrees Celsius in the shade again. At checkpoint after checkpoint, we were treated with grudging respect, and the day slid by.

At the town of Gedaref the road split in two, east to the Red Sea and south to Ethiopia. Gedaref was also the last chance to fill fuel and water tanks; from here on it would be bush, a dirt road, small villages and bandits. It felt decidedly unreal. Trouble started as soon as we hit the outskirts of town—the petrol station manager said our permits weren't valid. Arguing wasn't working and neither was gentle persuasion, but we had a stroke of luck. By chance, a senior official was at the police checkpoint on the road, and he authorized the permits with a wonderful flourishing signature.

The next morning we found three tracks heading south across the sand, but no signposts. The townspeople didn't seem to understand us when we asked for directions. All we could do was take a compass bearing and head off down the track that seemed to be the best bet. The beige sand and sparse growth gently changed to black earth and scrubby bush. Most of Sudan is a flat, featureless plain that covers great latitude—it's the size of France plus a good chunk of Spain. I'd read that, for all its miles of desert, vast acres in fact were fertile enough to produce tremendous quantities of food. The missing element was water in regular supply.

The soil in the corners of the track had been pounded into a fine, deep dust by the heavily overloaded trucks that kept the villages supplied and acted as the local bus service. The battle for us was the combination of deep ruts still left from the last rains and soft, thick pockets of dust that would instantly suck power. They were rather like riding into baths full of talcum powder, but I was glad that the imminent rains hadn't started; this section would have been a black quagmire.

Suddenly there were five tracks diverging ahead of us, three of which could have been right. The road conditions were making the bikes drink fuel much quicker than I'd thought possible, and the lack of shade in the intense heat was making sweat pour off us. We chose the wrong track, but didn't discover that for an hour. Going back and hoping to find the right turning was out of the question—it would eat too much time, fuel, and water. We decided the only choice was to ride through the chest-high, scrubby bush, try to miss picking up any thorns, and eventually come across the right track. The chase across the bush was a brain tease. Common sense kept saying to slow down, take it easy. A broken leg or indeed a broken bike at this stage would have been a disaster. But it was another "don't think about it" moment. Don't dwell—just go.

We found the right track at last, and soon we were at the halfway point to the border with Ethiopia. Doka was a large village surrounded by fields full of withered maize and a few bony cattle. It was packed with people and I realized that we'd crossed an invisible line: the local skin colours had changed from the light tans of the Arab world to the dark honey tans and Nubian jet of the south. Scrawny goats wandered around eating discarded orange peels, mango pits and even bits of old newspaper. The twenty or so huts were straw-roofed and walled with branches that had come from goodness knows where. I hadn't seen anything even remotely resembling a forest since arriving in Africa.

Conversations stopped dead as we rode across the bare, uneven, compacted dirt of the village centre. The Gedaref police had told us to report to the local cop shop, which was another straw-roofed hut. The police chief was dressed in a djellaba which did nothing to hide his girth. A young lad was shifting the air around the inside of the station with a palm frond mat that was suspended from the roof beams. The policeman didn't seem especially surprised to see us. In the corner sat a large army-type radio, so we guessed that he'd been warned that three crazies were heading in his direction.

The police chief's manner was rather benevolent and completely authoritative. Around him sat a collection of men who had the manner of courtiers attending the king. To our delight, there wasn't a trace of the aggression we'd found in Gedaref.

He questioned us in a rich baritone which suited his bulk perfectly:

"Why are you riding together?"

"Are you married?" (This, of course, was said to Mike and Sally, with a grin and a wobble of his belly.)

"How big are the engines on your motorcycles?"

"How much fuel and water can you carry?"

"Have you liked Sudan?"

"We don't see people like you. Why do you want to go to Ethiopia?"

"Do you have a gun?"

This kind of interrogation worked! I suspected that he always managed to get more information out of people than the abrupt, demanding police in Gedaref did.

We seemed to have the right answers to his questions. He smiled, but then concern slipped across his face. "You will have to travel to the border in a truck convoy. Bandits for you are now, to my very great regret, a serious problem." The men in the hut nodded in unison at this.

The trouble was that convoys were few and far between, and a wait of several days in the village was not something we wanted to experience. We hadn't much time left on our Sudanese visas, and the big worry was still the imminent rainy season, which could hit at any moment.

But it turned out our luck was in—the local tribal chief's oldest son and a princess from a neighbouring region were getting married that day. People had walked or travelled by truck for days to show their respect, and a wedding convoy would be leaving from the village at some time later that day. The bad news, when we thought about it, was that, according to Africa time, "sometime later that day" could well turn into "much later that day."

Riding in the dark on these roads didn't seem to be a good idea. I imagined thick dust in my headlights, making it even harder still to see where the next hole or rock was. The police chief was obviously on the ball, though, and read the worry on our faces. He decided to let us go the final stage on our own.

Absolutely delighted, we scooted out of the village.

After just ten minutes, we took the wrong track again. The sun was beginning to fall and once again we were faced with the same set of problems: fuel, water, and time—not to mention bandits. This time our luck was really in: there, on the horizon, was a man herding goats. He stood leaning on his long black staff, standing absolutely still with an unperturbed expression on his face. It seemed almost as if it were completely natural for him to see two dirty, large, and overloaded motorbikes thumping across his world.

Now we only had to make him understand what we wanted. The next village down the road that we should have been on was called Maliha. Perhaps if we pronounced this in as many ways as we could manage, then at least one of them would be close to the mark. Finally running out of variations, we were beginning to feel a bit desperate.

"I do speak perfectly good English, you know," he suddenly told us in an excellent Oxford English accent. "If you ride for half a mile in that direction, you will come to the road. Go left on it."

Feeling decidedly silly, we asked how he spoke such good English. It turned out that he'd been studying in England and was the son of a wealthy chief. His father and older brother had been killed in a truck accident, which had left him head of the family. To get back in touch with his "old world," he'd decided to herd goats for a couple of weeks.

The landscape was changing from scrubby, flat bushland to rolling hills. In the distance were the blues and greens of mountains—Ethiopia. As the sun dropped further towards the horizon, I noticed the silhouettes of armed soldiers standing on the hilltops. In one way they were a comfort, but also they were a sharp reminder that we really were in a dodgy part of the world. If everything hadn't been happening so quickly, perhaps I would have been scared.

A whiff of wood smoke was the first hint that we were approaching a small village, then we were greeted by the bizarre sight of a crowd of people, men, women and children lining the road. They were dressed from head to toe in pure white robes and white turbans; black Arabic lettering decorated the long white banners that they were waving on poles. When the people saw us, the women started to ululate. Their high-pitched wailing seemed to rise and fall in an odd sort of harmony, and was clearly audible even over the noise of the bike and through my helmet. The crowd parted as we rode closer, and then the people swarmed around us. With obvious pride, a tray of purple-coloured drinks was proffered. It was one of those situations where refusal might well have offended. The juice was diluted pomegranate, and delicious, but after seeing the last village's water supply I wondered how long it would be before I fell ill. We thanked them as best we could and rode on, leaving a strangely confused crowd behind us.

The road continued to get rockier and the hills higher. At the next village we were greeted in much the same fashion, but this time a bellowing cow was dragged out in front of us. To our horror, its throat was cut with a large curved sword. Blood spurted out across the road and we kept on going. It was a little bit too bizarre for us to linger.

The last thirty kilometres to the border town went by in a weary haze. By now I was tired, thirsty, and looking forward to whatever hotel the border might be able to offer. I didn't really care how bad it might be. We would try to cross the border in the morning.

Once again, white-robed people greeted us at the edge of the village, but this time there were lots of soldiers around, many of them officers. The crowd excitedly swirled around us, but suddenly the atmosphere changed. An army convoy had pulled into the village, and in the second jeep sat a brigadier wearing dress uniform and an angry face. An officer hurried up our tire tracks.

"You leave now," he ordered.

The only place to go was the local hotel down a rough back road. There weren't any rooms, just an enclosed space with rough wooden beds arranged around the edges. It would do. We'd been up and battling with the day for almost eleven hours. A wash, several cups of tea, and a feed were needed. As we relaxed, we congratulated ourselves on making it through the day without any serious mishaps, and started to wonder what the next day would bring.

Suddenly the rough wooden gate swung open and in rushed a group of soldiers who made it quite obvious that we were no longer welcome. They kept pointing towards the south and the only understandable word was "Ethiopia."

We were finding out what the results of "raining on someone's parade" were all about. It was the brigadier's parade we'd ruined, and he was mightily pissed. He'd apparently travelled from Khartoum to open a new hospital; we'd stolen his thunder all the way for hours.

With no choice but to leave, we rode from the newly whitewashed walls of the Sudanese border post into Ethiopia and a crowd of teenagers in disintegrating camouflage uniforms. Rifles and AK-47s were pointing in our direction and the noise was overwhelming. I had just time to think that an English speaker would be very nice to have around at that moment, and someone must have read my mind. There in front of us was a friendly face: "Do you need some help?" His English was broken but understandable.

As soon as we were talking, the tension of the crowd relaxed. Our new friend explained to the soldiers that we were tourists and had come to their country on holiday. I got the feeling that not only was he having to explain what tourists were, but was also struggling to explain what a holiday was. Twenty years of war had officially ended just a few weeks before, so most of these kids had never seen people like us. A Martian landing on Earth for the first time would probably get the same reaction.

Guns were still pointing at us as our translator led the way through the crowd and along the dirt track that doubled as the border town's main street. The huts along the edges were in a ramshackle state, and the village goats and dogs looked as if they were not long for this world. The track itself was rutted and full of rubbish. The troops' post wasn't in any better condition. The soldiers pushed us towards a hut and indicated that we were to wait inside.

Moments later there was gunfire, shouting and screaming out in the street. The upside of the shooting was that it woke up the Captain. This guy, in total contrast to his troops, was a very snappy dresser, and to our relief he spoke a little English. On his head sat a clean red beret whose badge was a shiny skull. His uniform was a well-pressed pale green and even his belt and boots held a high gloss. I knew that I looked as filthy as I felt.

The gist of the captain's questions was, "What on earth were we doing at this border?" With one ear on what was still rumbling outside and the other on our friendly jabber, he inspected our passports … upside-down. I could see him mentally tossing a coin.

"All right, all right, you can go," he said.

Fantastic! We climbed aboard the bikes and rode out of the village before he could change his mind.

I don't actually remember much about the next hours; I must have been on some sort of physical and mental overdrive. But I do remember the wildly coloured birds that kept darting across the road, which was in far better condition than it had been on the Sudanese side. We swooped on, swirling dust behind us as we passed burnt-out army trucks and tanks. Fords over deep, dry riverbeds told the tale of the road in the rainy season, confirming that our decision to press on had been right.

Around us, the low forest grew ever denser and finally we reached a village. The sun was about ten minutes away from dropping below the hillsides. Once again, we were a conversation-stopper. In fact, many of the people ran away to hide behind the huts. The first to come out was a child and it was he who clicked the fastest to our badly-accented Anglo-Amharic version of "Where is the hotel?"

He ran off in front of the bikes, leading us down a dirt track into the inevitable stick enclosure. Inside this kraal was a collection of wood, thatch, mud, and hide buildings that seemed to have been stitched together with bits of old string and wire. The people looked baffled, scared and bewildered—two motorcycles had just ridden into their living room! But yes, this was the village hotel.

At that moment, the sun finally disappeared.

I was too tired to check the bike for any loosened nuts and bolts or to clean the air filter as I knew I should. We ate and drank, and then I tumbled onto the bed, as totally exhausted as I'd ever been. I fell asleep listening to the sounds of donkeys braying in the enclosure, a radio playing distinctive Ethiopian music, and a cock crowing (on Africa time). The day had been a very long sixteen hours. Then I remembered where I was, and nothing else mattered. We were in Ethiopia. We'd made it!

Sam Manicom motorcycled around the world for 8 years, covering 200,000 miles and visiting 55 countries. He is the author of four travel books, Into Africa; Under Asian Skies; Distant Suns; *and* Tortillas to Totems. *He freelances travel articles for magazines around the world.*

Sam's books are available in paperback and e-book formats with his first two books now released as audiobooks.

Web: Sam-Manicom.com
Twitter: @SamManicom

Adventure Trio: The Great Divide or Bust!

Sandy Borden

After a year of planning and mapping, rebuilds and tune-ups, in the summer of 2012 we were ready to tackle the Great Divide, an iconic ride in the States that stretches from the Mexico/New Mexico line to the Montana/Canada border. As a motorcycling family of three, we're used to going with the flow, staying away from a schedule. But this year, we strayed from our norm and made promises to press and TV alike, allowing our commitments to others to guide us instead of sticking with our usual groove. It almost broke us. Almost. What transpired during our four-week trek to conquer the Great Divide was a hard lesson, but one that we needed to learn.

We've been travelling as a family on BMWs (with Jack riding pillion on the back of Terry's 2006 BMW GSA and me riding sweep with my 2003 BMW F650 GS) since 2007, when Jack was just six years old. Our in-helmet radios keep us in constant contact, calling out safety stops, bathroom breaks, and distracted drivers. Each summer we venture off on a grand escape, doing our best to carve out an extra couple of days, sometimes a week, in hopes of creating more spectacular memories. Summers off from the suburban school schedule mean it's time to flee the usual, leaving work and home behind, to experience something beyond the trips to

Costco and playdates. We've tackled Canada twice, riding to Kamloops in British Columbia during a particularly damp June in 2011. We've chased snow flurries and rain clouds through the west, tornadoes and thunderstorms through the plains. Jack has experienced more of Mother Nature's wrath and beauty in his 11 years than most of us will see in a lifetime.

Always a willing passenger, at 11 Jack was ready to take on another off-road challenge. (The lack of proper protective gear for Jack had kept us from hitting the road sooner, as we would not take to the pavement until our pillion was fully covered. While there is plenty of dirt-riding gear to outfit little ones, no one had made a full motorcycle riding suit until BMW came out with the Stoke Suit, a miniature version of an adult riding suit, complete with full padding and zippers to let out extra material as the kiddo grows.)

Like many adventurous Americans, we had had the Great Divide on our "to do" list for several years. Many people have written about their Divide experiences, whether via two feet, two wheels, or vehicle, and with each article we read about this historic journey, the more we knew we had to take it on, Adventure Trio-style. Could we do it as a family of three on two motorcycles? Only by attempting it could we answer that question. So, after we wrapped up the previous summer's four-week trip, we decided that the Divide was going to be our next challenge. This was committing to a major undertaking of dirt, gravel, and silt. Terry was already riding a heavy bike; a growing Jack and camping gear were going to add both weight and challenge. We knew we had to gear down even further, taking as much weight as possible off of each bike. Remember, we're packing for three individuals. That means three times the clothing, camping gear, and food. Fortunately, we had just purchased three new, much more compact bedrolls. That was a major find in our quest to reduce the bulk of Terry's U-shaped duffel. We also abandoned the camp pillows. Our clothing stuff-sacks were going to have to pull extra duty. I had just switched my "kitchen" top case to the GIVI TRK46N, making it lighter, more user-friendly, and easier to pack. I had also eliminated a duffel bag, making my bike less top-heavy and more maneuverable. But on this trip, we were carrying something new—camera gear. We had a goal to shoot footage of our trip, creating a travel documentary for The Ted Simon Foundation. There was a lot riding on our shoulders, as well as our bikes.

When you ride as a family, you add a new, very personal variable to the mix of things that may affect your trip: you are taking your child on the road via two wheels. While this may not be the first choice for many families who like to travel, it's certainly not out of the question. Some people have told us our mode of transportation is "dangerous," but we find it much more dangerous to cram a family into a small car and ask them to be patient for the next six to eight hours.

Jack is our decision-maker when it comes to pressing on or staying put. He is our rational voice in questionable moments. Knowing that the heat of the summer was going to be upon us, we made the decision to bypass the New Mexico portion of the ride. Asking our little man to bear the Arizona heat on our journey east just to say "We did it!" was unfair. To be honest, this was a bit hard for me and Terry. We wanted to say we did the entire route "just like everybody else." But we needed to remember one thing—we are not like everybody else.

The wildfires of 2012 in New Mexico and Colorado became a major issue for us, as the Divide route took us right smack into the middle of that war zone. By the time we made it to South Fork, Colorado, the fires were ravaging half of the state and most of the Divide. Smoke from a new fire just north of us poured into the valley, blocking out the sun and casting a shadow on our already tattered spirits. Thick smoke hung like a grey curtain across the valley and singed our lungs with each inhalation, and to me it felt like the pain and sorrow of the residents and firefighters fighting this ever-growing rage flowed in, too, reminding the three of us just how lucky we were.

By a week into the trip, we had already had to scrap most of the southern portion of the Divide. To take a chance and brave the thick smoke and possibility of yet another fire starting would have been unwise. At no time were we going to put ourselves at risk. The heat was also becoming an issue. Anywhere below 8,500 feet promised temperatures of 90 degrees plus. Unlike last summer's chilly, rainy conditions, we were in the midst of a heat wave with no end in sight. Even with all our planning, we couldn't escape Mother Nature's wrath.

As we holed up for yet another night in a cabin, Jack declared, "I don't even feel like we're on our trip. We haven't done enough camping."

Indeed, young squire.

The next morning, we headed north on Highway 149 with stunning views of the San Juan Mountains, their rocky formations jutting out of the landscape, greeting us through the turns with a constant flood of smoke reminding us of what lay ahead. The goal was to set up camp for a night, then head to the Divide. We were determined to hit the dirt NO MATTER WHAT. We didn't know it, but we were losing our way. The "have-to" commitments we had made at the beginning of our journey were beginning to win over the "want-to"s.

We found the ideal spot to set up camp just outside of Almont, Colorado, along the Taylor River, its chilly temperature reminding us just how cold a snow-fed rush of water can be. Jack took the chance to break out his fishing rod while Terry and I set out to plan the rest of our route. But the beauty that surrounded us was not enough to break the bad juju. Each of us was unhappy, yet no one was willing to be the first to admit it. Instead of taking our time and enjoying the journey, we found ourselves worrying about having enough footage, how to manage an impending interview, and sticking with the original plan. This was not us and, very soon, one of us was going to crack. And then, it happened.

I was the first to blow. It wasn't pretty. I raged out in a fit of screams and accusations, launching our map book several feet from camp. Terry followed suit, matching my rage with more yelling and the flinging of yet another inanimate object into space. I was convinced that we were done, that we needed to pack up and head home first thing in the morning. Our year of planning and promises to others had come to this: our need to "ride it like everybody else" had broken us. There were tears ... lots. There were battles upon battles. But the biggest battle was within ourselves. We had allowed ourselves to be led astray from what works for us as a family. We had put each other at risk emotionally just to please the media masses. This was a turning point for our Trio. We could choose to leave everyone else behind and take our trip back, or we could hang our helmets in defeat and head west.

We took it back.

With the dawn came a renewed feeling of empowerment. We had escaped the dark cloud and made the decision as a family to press north and make it ours. The first decision—NO MORE PLANNING! We always tell others that the plan is to have no plan. We had gone against our own golden rule. Second—put the electronics down. No more putting commitments to others before ourselves. We pushed back our interview and put our energy into each other. Third—so what if we don't ride the whole Great Divide?! Terry and I had allowed ourselves to be swallowed up in this notion that unless you ride the whole Divide, you're not a true Divide rider. We took a step back, assessed the situation and made one clear decision—unless you come together and communicate honestly, you're not a true team. We are a team, and we are Divide riders. Maybe not the whole Divide, not this time, but that was okay. We were going to do it our way.

After dodging the fires and surviving the heat, the time had come to join the Divide route. We picked it up in Northern Colorado, just outside of Steamboat Springs. Finally! I made sure to hop off the bike and do a victory dance. The Running Man IS possible when fully geared up.

Rawlins, Wyoming, was our next pickup point for the Divide. It was also going to prove to be our longest day in the dirt. After a left turn off of Highway 287, we rode over 120 miles of gravel, silt, and sand and not once did Jack complain. He rode it like he owned it. We saw only one truck the entire day. Herds of antelope attempted to race Terry's bike, while free-range cattle dotted the landscape. It was a battle between GPS maps and paper maps, each proving themselves useful at different junctions. After a long day on the pegs, we rolled into Atlantic City, Wyoming, an old mining and cowboy town. We pulled up at a restaurant that advertised fresh Rocky Mountain oysters. We were half a plate into said oysters when we 'fessed up to Jack what they REALLY were. He shot us a look of disbelief, shrugged his shoulders, and reached for another slice. Amazing how good some things can taste with just a little more hot sauce. We toasted to Jack and his willingness to take it as it comes. Good on ya, big guy.

The rest of our journey found us on and off the trail, picking it up as the weather and the little man dictated. Some days Jack didn't want to be bounced around in the dirt, and that was okay. We didn't make it further north than Wyoming, and that's fine with us. The dream of riding the Great Divide from Mexico to Canada was not to be this year. We had covered a chunk of Colorado and all of Wyoming, just kissing the Montana border.

As we headed home, we were feeling a bit defeated, yet proud of all that we had encountered during this time. And that's what it means to be part of this Trio team. We almost lost our spirit. We almost lost our vision. Could you imagine what would have happened if we had succumbed to defeat and headed home? What a tragedy that would've been! Jack would have learned that in tough times, you just throw up your arms and admit defeat. Instead, he learned that when you lose your way, you come together to find a solution. It may be a little trickier when you're travelling on two wheels, but doesn't that make it more exciting? Adventure motorcycle travel is the beauty of the unknown. When you do adventure motorcycle travel as a family, it truly is beautiful.

Sandy Borden is a writer and the most feminine member of the Adventure Trio. Sandy, Terry and Jack have been travelling as a family of three on two BMW motorcycles since Jack was just six years old. Their travels have taken them throughout North America, Canada and Mexico as well as Central and South America.

Web: AdventureTrio.com
Twitter: @AdventureTrio

Just One for the Road!

Paddy Tyson

The earthen road fell away sharply through a switchback corner and disappeared into the flowing water.

I switched off the bike and thought about how, in times past, I would have settled down and rolled a cigarette during moments just like this. I'd have considered the situation, taken stock, drawn heavily, and maybe blown a smoke ring or two in a desire to convince myself I was cool and unperturbed by another river crossing. But not now.

The surrounding scrubby eucalyptus forest provided a silvery-green contrast to the otherwise ochre earth of the harsh Australian outback. It was an earth which had penetrated every part of my clothing and was baked between the fins of my engine. This would be an excellent opportunity to wash the bike and get a little respite from the heat, were it not for the signs on the water's edge warning of saltwater crocodiles.

I hadn't seen another vehicle all day, and yet someone had gone to the trouble of erecting a sign by the ford that warned all passengers to remain within their vehicle while in or near the water. Come to think of it, I hadn't even seen another road sign in the previous couple of hundred kilometres. Clunky old German MZ motorcycles may be solidly built, but even they can't protect a tasty passenger from the jaws of an interested saltie.

I looked at the sign and then into the water. The first three or four metres of the crossing looked as though it was about thigh-deep, but the water was clear to the boulder-strewn bottom. The following ten metres appeared less than knee-deep, but on either side of the ford, the over-hanging foliage created so many shadows that my croc-spotting skills felt a little compromised. (In truth, they weren't well-practiced skills.) Rather than roll a cigarette, I decided to have a crap in the bushes as a moment of contemplation. I'd think about my predicament: to cross, or not. I didn't have the fuel to retrace my route.

I've never been a hero, but always thought heroic acts should have an audience greater than a handful of Northern Territory cockatoos. This was 2003, so I wasn't concerned my gruesome death would fail to become a YouTube sensation, but I'd always hoped news of any untimely demise would at least make my local paper so friends didn't think I was avoiding them.

My silent musing was rocked by a Toyota pickup crashing through the undergrowth, upturned alloy dinghy strapped on at a jaunty angle. A tattooed, sun-weathered arm dangled from the window, tinnie in hand. A swarthy antipodean head leaned out to admire my position.

"G'day, mate! Takin' a dump? Bonza bike. Amphibious, is it?"

"Ah, yes. Hello. I was just considering the crossing actually, and that warning sign about salties."

"Shit, mate, there's no crocs here, that's just for the bloody tourists."

Heart-warmed by this local knowledge, I took comfort in the offer of a cold beer from his colleague. Well, why not? It was over thirty degrees; I'd drunk little all day and hadn't eaten at all. With the first few gulps, I could feel the alcohol coursing through the blood vessels in my brain. The pounding felt good. As blokes do, we discussed my bike, the trip I was on, the depth of the water, where I was heading, the economy of the bike, the depth of the water again … All as I gently swayed and pleasantly tingled.

A decision was made that we'd all wade through to gauge the depth; that I'd carry my roll bag and the guys would carry one pannier each. I was getting braver and figured if we all went in together, my odds were improved and I'd have a one-in-three chance if a croc was hungry.

Once the first transit was complete, we had another tinnie. The joy of successfully tackling the obstacle mixed with my growing alcoholic euphoria, and our conversation developed, but my new friends didn't tell me much about themselves. In rudimentary outback style they fashioned an exhaust bung from detritus in the back of the ute and, second beer finished, we all pushed the bike through. Emboldened by the booze, I feared nothing, but revelled in the cool water in my boots and up my legs. This was adventure the likes of which I'd read about—Ewan and Charley had yet to make a movie. The bike remained upright to the other side.

With a taste for the amber nectar, I darted back through the water for just one more out of the cool-box and to retrieve my jacket and lid. I had fewer than 80 kilometres before my planned stop for the night, where I knew there was fuel. The feeling of liberation that accompanies a complete disregard for another nation's road traffic laws is irresponsible in the extreme but hard to beat, especially somewhere as remote and hot as northern Australia. I looked across the river at my iron horse stood on the far riverbank, ready to take me on through the wilderness to my next challenge. Damn, I felt good!

I asked the lads for news of the road ahead and the size of the five other river crossings on my map. All were smaller, they said, but who cared, I could tackle them alone. I yelled my thanks as they fired up their Toyota, and then one last parting shot:

"But what are you guys doing out here anyway?"

"Shit, mate, we're hunting crocs!"

Like seeing a ghost, the chill ran through me and I looked across the water again to my bike and all my worldly belongings on the other side. What was that in the shadows? Had the water always been tumbling over that rock? I reassessed the whole scene. Could a simple stretch of crystal-clear water suddenly transform into a sea patrolled by prehistoric monsters of the deep? That, it seemed, might depend on how much beer I'd consumed.

I pulled myself together, waded in, and began singing a little song. Safely on the other side, I threw caution to the wind and deemed it too hot for a helmet as I climbed aboard the bike; the alcohol was making my emotions swing like a pendulum. The soaking had meant nothing to either me or the bike—the 500cc single thudded into life as normal, taking me over the alluvial plain to the next finger of the inappropriately named Alligator River.

The hard red earth was now pebble-strewn, the surface gouged with washouts exposing tree roots, but we bumbled along, pleasantly numb to the more conventional dangers of motorcycling until the second crossing appeared, neither as wide nor as deep as the first. I parked up and went for a wade, comforted by the fact that there were no warning signs. Having grown up in a culture where one wouldn't dare walk on a lawn if a sign forbade it, I was guided by the legitimacy of their absence as I merrily considered my best route through. Engine running and in gear for drive, I walked along beside the bike, holding it against the current. And we were through. Too easy! I could almost taste dinner.

In a handful of kilometres I was at it again; this was an even smaller crossing and one I could ride. Ha ha! Still nearly two hours of daylight and, by my reckoning, hardly 60 kilometres to go. I upped the pace. The crocs were history, the track was manageable, the bike was running well, my abilities were clearly invincible, and my desire for another beer was palpable.

Down a tunnel of vegetation another pathetic stream appeared, maybe five metres wide, but engulfed in shadow. The water was pleasantly calm. The heat remained intense, so I slowed on approach and then went for the cooling spray option, gently opening the throttle in second gear. I was in control and it felt good. No croc would dare take me on now, nor would those pesky, scaly dinosaurs keep me from my dinner.

They didn't need to.

As the indicators, headlight, and then clocks disappeared into that calm, deep water hole, everything changed.

Paddy Tyson is a wandering Irishman who has been travelling the world by motorcycle since 1991. He writes for various motorcycle publications in the UK and North America and provides light-hearted entertainment for those willing to sit through a presentation of earlier travels. Previously a lecturer, journalist, political campaigner and dispatch rider, he now edits Overland *and is an advisor for The Ted Simon Foundation and a director of Shuvvy Press Ltd. He drinks an inordinate amount of tea. Paddy is the author of* The Hunt for Puerto Del Faglioli: A Motorcycle Adventure in Search of the Improbable.

Web: PaddyTyson.com
Web: OverlandMag.com

The Sweet Science

Neil Peart

The following is an adapted extract from Far and Near: On Days Like These, *published by ECW Press (ECWpress.com). Used with permission. Editor's Note: This material has been altered for length. Any incongruity or jarring transitions are to be blamed on Oscillator Press ... those jerks.*

The Sweet Science. The phrase was coined a couple of hundred years ago by an English sportswriter, referring to ... boxing.

This reporter has never sensed anything "sweet" or "scientific" about a couple of guys punching each other's lights out, but some people feel it. Among the many superb non-fiction writers to have appeared serially in *The New Yorker* over the years (Joseph Mitchell, Dorothy Parker, Truman Capote, John McPhee, etc.), A.J. Liebling revived the theme for a series of articles about boxing in the 1930s and '40s that were later collected in a book titled *The Sweet Science* (1956).

Personally, I can think of human activities that seem infinitely sweeter than pugilism (though the Greek word is fun—*pygmachia*—but perhaps not as fun as *eros),* and others that are more truly scientific. Even, dare I say, more *artful.* And without causing facial mutilation and irreversible brain damage.

One late April day on my motorcycle, railing through the forested mountains of North Carolina on a relentless sequence of curves in every possible geometry, I thought, "*This* is the sweet science."

Threading a series of corners like this with sporting intent (i.e., swiftly and smoothly), a great many decisions are made and executed. You choose your entry speed and gear early, get the bike settled before you bank it in, and keep to the outside of the lane as long as you can, to see through the corner as far as possible and into the next one—and *be* seen by any oncoming traffic. Turn in early toward the apex, always allowing a little leeway to adjust your line, speed, or banking angle to dodge a pothole, a spray of gravel, an oncoming vehicle wandering into your lane, or—on blind rural corners—a tractor or a cow. With everything in balance, once you're committed to the turn and in a steady state, a few degrees more or less throttle should be all the steering you need. To adjust the lean angle is to adjust the radius of the arc.

Exiting the turn, you run out wide again, head turned to look through the next corner (a counterintuitive technique that has to be *learned*: "Don't look where you are, look where you're *going*").

The science of physics rules everything here, perhaps most of all where the rubber meets the road—the so-called coefficient of friction (COF, or μ)—where your tires roll on pavement, gravel, dirt, wet leaves, manure, or puddles. On a motorcycle, you experience no "lateral Gs"—the rider always feels ninety degrees of gravitational pull, and is never thrown from side to side as one would be in a car.

However, the corollary is that a motorcycle has a very small contact patch—virtually two handprints gripping the road—and it is a "single-track" vehicle. It has been said that, "A motorcycle is so stupid it can't even stand up by itself." That is a mantra to be kept in mind at all times. (My friend Rick Foster adds another groaner: "A motorcycle can't stand up by itself—because it's two-tired.")

At its best, the rider's rhythm through a series of corners is like a slalom course on skis, or a hot lap on a racetrack—linking the turns gracefully, smoothly, and safely. No doubt the experience is sharpened by constant awareness of the *consequences*. Getting it right is very satisfying; getting it wrong could be very painful.

Tour itineraries vary almost infinitely in the way show dates are connected and ordered—and thus in the areas between that I am able to explore on days off. The early dates on one recent tour happened to fall such that I was able to route us through North Carolina on several consecutive days off, commuting among shows in Orlando, Nashville, Raleigh, and Virginia Beach. Thus, by lucky happenstance, North Carolina became my "new discovery." (A few tours ago I told Geddy that my latest discovery was Pennsylvania, and he said, "I'm pretty sure it's already been discovered—people live there and that.")

Previously I have rhapsodized about riding in other East Coast regions such as Virginia, West Virginia, and upstate New York, but this time the mountain back roads of North Carolina greatly impressed me. They gave Michael and me a rich and varied playground—I mean *scientific laboratory*.

One theme I have been pursuing in our photo setups is seeing how many corners we can get into one scene. Extreme settings, like a series of steep switchbacks in the Alps or Andes (see *Far and Away's* "The Power of Magical Thinking"), make it easy, but "regular" mountain roads are more of a challenge.

One of those North Carolina byways made our highest score so far—five curves in one shot. It will be hard to beat, not just numerically, but for the road's lack of shoulders, power lines, guardrails, or other unsightly distractions. As I ride along with an eye out for photo settings, countless possibilities are rejected simply for having ugly power lines in them—a deal-breaker for me. (Yes, I know there are easy ways to "fix it in the mix," as musicians used to say, and that's fine for "decorative" photos. But not for "scientific" ones. We have our standards.)

Another science of paramount importance to a motorcyclist is meteorology—the *weather*. (As a weather enthusiast, I confess that that seems like a sweet science, too.) Unlike passengers in a car, a motorcycle rider is exposed to every degree of temperature, every drop of precipitation, and every unsettling crosswind. I have noted before that on the motorcycle, I can feel a rise or fall of only two degrees, and of course the difference between riding on a wet or dry road surface changes *everything*. Temperature and moisture have a direct effect not only on one's comfort level, but on that all-important physical relationship with the road.

Traction, control, margin of error, not falling down.

Then there is the "vision" thing, to see and be seen. Clearly (or not), the weather has much to do with that, as well ….

This first leg of the second part of the *Clockwork Angels* tour, in spring 2013, had been designed to be an East Coast run. However, late last year the band was informed that our presence might be required at some little awards show on the West Coast, in mid-April.

At the time, the odds of us being inducted into the Rock and Roll Hall of Fame seemed unlikely to absurd, after something like fourteen years of rejection, but apparently we were "on the ballot." So manager Ray insisted we had to factor it into our plans, and adjustments had to be made.

One change that suited me was that instead of band rehearsals taking place in Toronto, as usual, they would be in Los Angeles, so I would have a few extra weeks at home. In December, I got a message from Ray asking me to call him. Fearing bad news (we get our share of that, like anyone else), I called him with a little trepidation. When Ray told me we were "in," it took a while to process the mix of feelings: disbelief, delight, and a little *more* trepidation. There would be … challenges … (See "Where Words Fail, Music Speaks.")

Following my own pre-tour preparations at the local Y, and at Drum Channel's studio (two and a half weeks of playing along with the recorded versions of the show, tuning up my technique and stamina), I joined the Guys at Work (Alex, Geddy, and our crew) at a warehouse in the San Fernando Valley.

That was when things started to become surreal.

On our last day in the warehouse, we were joined by Dave Grohl and Taylor Hawkins from the Foo Fighters, and our mutual co-producer Nick "Booujzhe" Raskulinecz. They wanted to rehearse a spoof of us from … thirty-six years ago.

By now, the televised show in all its glory (I have faith it will retain the essence of what it was like to experience the real-time event—a truly larger-than-life experience) has been widely shared. The performances, the speeches, the humour, and the overwhelming gathering of the Great and the Good are part of some kind of history now. However, the inner experience of living all that was something else again. Not larger than life, but exactly life-size.

Now—back to business-as-usual for us Rushians. First full-production rehearsal tonight, then again tomorrow night, then a day off, then the first show.

Then some more shows ....

On that subject, one photo that reached me by chance seemed to tell a nice story—because it is a true fan's-eye-view, a random moment from a random place in the crowd. Typically, it was captured on one of the thousands of cellphone cameras we see out there every night. (Some people seem to spend half the show looking through, or at, their handheld devices.) Matt Scannell asked me to arrange a pair of tickets for a friend of his at one of our shows, and later, the friend sent Matt his thanks, and a photo, taken by his guest. I like to leave it anonymous, as a symbol of something that seems important. I am always playing for somebody named "A. Fan." Perhaps an ideal listener I consider The Fan.

It also captures a moment I wrote about in a previous story—the cello players hunched over their instruments to protect them from the heat of the pyrotechnics. (I told Jacob he is rocking a Chuck Berry pose.)

The show this time out is the same musically and visually as the one we performed last fall—thirty-five times—so you could say we "have it down." While that's true, the performance is never easy, and because of that, it remains rewarding to get it right—to feel that I'm getting the sweet science of drumming smooth and strong.

And even after all those shows, before starting certain especially complicated songs, like "Grand Designs" or "Headlong Flight," for example, or before one of my solo spots, I pause to engage a higher gear of concentration. Some songs I can just count in and launch, but those examples demand just a little more attention to detail.

Some roads are like that, too. Sometimes you have a relaxed cruise, an easy flow down a straight, open road. In the mountain roads of North Carolina, you need a little more attention to detail, a higher gear of concentration ....

If motorcycling is science, travelling is art. Getting from one place to another independently, with a sense of adventure and appreciation, requires a creative vision, technical experience, and, perhaps most of all, adaptability.

The high concept is "What is the most excellent thing I can do today?" but it must sometimes yield to realities like time and distance, weather and traffic, or even just getting to work on time. Because sometimes work is the most excellent thing I can do today, and I can only try to embellish the work with some recreation and exploration.

Neil Peart is the drummer and lyricist for an "up-and-coming" Canadian band called RUSH. This Rock and Roll Hall of Famer is an avid motorcyclist, and the author of several books, including Ghost Rider; Traveling Music; Far and Near; Far and Away; Roadshow; *and* The Masked Rider.

Web: NeilPeart.com

Riding in the Rain

Jeremy Kroeker

"Good morning, sunshine!" I said, throwing open the shutters of my hotel room and staring into swirling fog. I had always suspected that *The Secret* was bullshit, and here was my proof.

Dark rows of vines in a nearby field faded into grey. Even the structures on the edge of the vineyard seemed depressed. In neighbouring Austria, they had white houses with decorative wooden beams and billows of flowers at every window. Here in Slovenia, the buildings distinguished themselves from the mist only insofar as they were cube-like.

Water hissed to a boil on my camp stove and I poured myself a cup of instant coffee. While waiting for it to cool, I wondered when I would ever see the sun. Since landing in Germany with my motorcycle, a tired KLR 650, I had ridden in the rain every day for a week. My jacket smelled of rotten milk for some reason, and my fingers were black from the dye in my gloves.

"Perhaps I could live out my days right here in this hotel," I thought, staring blankly out the window. But no. With a shake of my head, I turned to packing, hopeful that I would find my way to Croatia that afternoon.

With the back of my hand, I squeegeed drops of water off the seat. When the bike had warmed up, I hefted my leg onto the saddle, leaned forward, and slid into place.

On days like this, it's hard to tell if you're riding through light rain or thick fog. And it's important to make that distinction early if you hope to stay dry. Generally, your shins and knuckles feel damp if it's fog. If it's rain, you'll first notice water at your penis.

That's how I could tell the difference, anyway. My rain gear channeled water to the crotch. I thought of designing a filtration system that you could wear like an athletic cup, but where would the reservoir go? And the idea of a long straw seemed ... wrong. If I could just work out the bugs, though, I'd call it, "Purification Pants Rainwear," or just, "P-Pants."

By degrees, the mist began to exhibit all the characteristics of rain and I stopped to get out my waterproofs. I pulled on my trousers, knowing that I would soon have sloshing shorts. If only I had neoprene underwear, like a wetsuit. Then the water would gather warmth from my body and act as an insulating layer. But my shorts performed more like a G-suit worn by fighter pilots, the water rushing forward when braking, pooling in the rear upon acceleration. The result: constantly cold, shifting discomfort. At least I wouldn't black out if I had to deal with a bogey.

Then I picked up the gloves.

I tried slipping my hand into the first glove, but it wouldn't go. The liner stuck to my skin and wadded up at the fingers like a bunch of tampons.

Pulling harder on the cuff, I tugged at the glove with staccato bursts, like a dog with a rope-toy. But my hand was trapped. I had worked up a sweat by this time and the perspiration made things worse. A ripple of claustrophobia began in my fingers and spread through my body from there.

Instinct failed me. My first thought was to whip the gloves into the ditch, rip off my clothing, and stand naked in the rain. Suppressing that reflex, I became very still. Rain spattered off my helmet and trickled down my neck as I took several deep breaths, each one rising to the up-lifted visor on my helmet and gathering there in beads of condensation.

After taking a moment to calm down, I snatched at the glove, as if trying to catch it off guard. This time I wiggled my fingers, probing for the proper channels as I pulled ever harder. Bit by bit, the glove yielded and I managed to seat it in place. I adjusted each finger until I was satisfied.

Then I took up my second glove.

Sometimes I imagine meeting the guy who designs raingear that can be neither donned nor doffed when wet. We both roll up at a gas station at about the same time. Of course, it's raining. When I figure out what he does for a job, rain gear designer, or whatever, I stop him right there by holding up an index finger.

"Just wait a minute," I say. Then I struggle to remove a waterlogged glove, shaking my head and laughing a bit because I know what's coming next.

Holding the glove by the cuff, I soggy-slap him in the face. "That's a sloggy!" I'd say (trademark), and I'd deliver it on behalf of us all.

How long this fantasy played out in my mind I can't say, but when I finally looked down, my body was wearing gloves. Now steaming with sweat on the inside while cold rain gathered in my shorts, I closed every-thing up and climbed back onto the bike.

That's when I realized that my keys were tucked inside a trouser pocket.

Faced with such circumstances in the past, I've been known to hop off the bike and sprint around in angry circles. But with age comes wisdom.

And so, with a sort of Zen calm that often follows unsustainable frustration, I took all the time I needed to remove my gloves, fish out the keys, replace the gloves, and ride away.

The wind drove the rain at me now and, as the temperature dropped, I retreated to a familiar state of mental and physical inactivity to better endure the suffering. I swept the road with my eyes rather than turning my head. I moderated my breathing, taking in slow, steady breaths. I froze in the saddle, knowing that even the slightest shift of body position would snap my mind back to horrible awareness.

When I could bear no more, I pulled in at a small coffee shop to warm up. I had some thermal underwear tucked away in my tank bag and I figured that it would do wonders to keep me warm, if not dry.

With all eyes in the crowded room fixed on me, I walked—squish-squish-squish—as directly as possible to the bathroom, leaving boot-sized puddles on the floor. The patrons turned to watch as I squeezed like a wet sponge through a narrow entry and shut the door.

Between the toilet and my magnetic tank bag, which clung to the metal radiator, only a few square feet of useable floor space remained—just enough room to stand in the spreading pool at my feet. I clambered onto the toilet for extra space, but the plastic seat was treacherous. When my feet slipped, I gave a shout as I caught myself against the wall. This would be a very stupid way to die.

Back on the floor, I braced myself against the door to remove my gaiters and outer rain booties, piling them on the ground to stand upon as a sort of Gore-Tex bath mat. To unlace my boots, I lifted each one up on to the toilet, dropping them to the ground with a splash and standing on them, too, on what was now the only dry patch in the room.

Fighting for balance, I thumped into the door while removing my pants, suddenly aware that only a thin, acoustically transparent barrier separated me from the quiet coffee shop. After some time I managed to shed my dripping underwear, replacing them with a pair of dry long johns.

When I had replaced enough clothing to reasonably step back into public view, I scooped up my belongings and prepared to squeeze outside. But when I reached for the handle, the door didn't budge. I jiggled the handle with increasing violence until the door rattled on its hinges. Then, just as I was about to kick my way into what would have been a dumbfounded coffee shop crowd, the door swung open as if nothing had happened.

I stood there facing everyone. A man coughed. Still clutching my wet clothes, I waved with my free hand. I didn't do it, but I wanted to go, "Tadaaaa!" We all stared at each other for a few seconds, but I kept my eyes on the floor as I walked to a table. Once I sat down, people lost interest. I pitied the next person who had to use the toilet, though.

And I pitied myself for when I had to leave. My gloves were off and the keys were in my pocket.

Jeremy Kroeker is the author of Motorcycle Therapy: A Canadian Adventure in Central America, *and* Through Dust and Darkness: A Motorcycle Journey of Fear and Faith in the Middle East. *With his motorcycle, he has traveled to 30 countries while managing to do at least one outrageously stupid thing in every one. He has evaded police in Egypt, tasted teargas in Israel, scrambled through minefields in Bosnia and Lebanon, and wrangled a venomous snake in Austria. One time he got a sliver in El Salvador.*

Web: MotorcycleTherapy.com

Twitter: @Jeremy_Kroeker

The Heart of Morocco

Issa Breibish

The view of Morocco's Rif Mountains from high on this stony perch is stunning. I'm up here with Bilay, my host for the evening. He often wanders up to this lookout, and it's easy to see why.

Somewhere just a few hundred feet below us, in a small cinder-block home, my wife Nita is recovering from a motorcycle crash—and from a heart that's forgotten how to beat properly. Her best hope for relief depended on my leaving the house, thus deflecting the attention of a family of hashish farmers so she could sleep.

Nita and I both crashed our motorcycles today, and we spent a few hours stranded on the side of a mountain pass while her heart beat out of control, but that all slips away up here. Even with the chill that accompanies the long tendrils of cloud above the marijuana hillsides, neither Bilay nor I wants to leave.

The distraction is a godsend.

* * *

Morocco, the easiest of the North African countries to travel, has become a petri dish of disaster for us, nurturing the growth of several disparate events into one massive cock-up. An exciting one hundred hours have passed since Nita's heart first showed signs of exploding in Spain and, with alarming regularity, new ingredients have continued to pour into the mix. Her irregular heartbeat brought on severe tunnel vision, then a cascading sweat, along with seized hands and feet—not a great combination for controlling a motorcycle.

Perhaps we should have taken the two hospital visits and ambulance rides in Almeria as bad omens. Instead, in what can only be described as delusional optimism, we just changed our ferry departure to the following day.

Then, at the border at Beni Ansar in Morocco, a stern man who looked like Saddam Hussein in an olive-drab onesie detained me for carrying cameras aboard my motorcycle. He feared that the tiny lenses had caught the commonplace corruption that tends to exist where officials hold power over people.

At the police station this simple misunderstanding escalated into accusations of spying and I felt the seriousness of our situation dawn on me for the first time. Thankfully, an hour of interrogation ended with a young officer demanding an oath on my mother's life that I hadn't filmed the border. Even after this surprising end to our detention, it appeared that Morocco's heart remained resistant to even our most sincere advances.

Next, food poisoning in Al Hoceima induced a gut-churning daze that led to a crash while navigating some switchbacks—my first crash on tarmac during our journey. As we climbed high into the Rif Mountains, expanding views of a green and brown patchwork valley filled our visors, while the path before us diminished almost entirely. Landslides had decimated sections of these gravel roads, leaving dirt tracks a couple of metres wide traversing long drops into the fields below. On either side, weathered peaks rose, forming rust-coloured and treeless walls that have acted as a natural barrier against outside interference for thousands of years.

But after I rode a steep, rocky track down from the hills that rejoined the tarmac just outside of the city, a tight right-hand turn up a four-foot ramp proved too much for my nausea-addled mind to coordinate. A motion we'd performed thousands of times before suddenly felt foreign enough to make me stab at the clutch like an over-eager novice. A moment later, from the vantage point of my backside, I watched the bike slide along the road before it came to rest about thirty feet away.

And then … nothing. Over the following hour on the road there was no chatter over the intercom headset. Not even the worry of a life-changing fall from the cliff could spark conversation from Nita. We soon learned that the excitement of my off had set the stage for her worst bout with Wolff-Parkinson-White syndrome yet, causing a short circuit that spun her heart into a furious gallop.

We stopped on the only flat surface we could find. Nita lay down in the dirt, with her head on a drybag and a view of the valley below that teased more than inspired. Her heart, now in full tachycardia, ran wild. It is hard to imagine a more helpless feeling than watching the desperation of a loved one trying to ease a stubborn heart. From the outside she appeared calm—almost at rest—but when I placed my hand on her back, I felt a soaked shirt, through which powerful thuds vibrated as her heart tried to correct itself. I felt useless.

After we had spent two hours motionless on the roadside, three men wearing Ferrari shirts and driving the smallest of cars rolled up. They insisted that we should spend the night in their home, just a few kilometres away.

Even in this short distance, however, we found time for one more crash. Emerging from a deep pit, Nita's bike shot straight into the air before lurching to the right and crashing down onto her leg in a way that left little doubt in my mind that my wife now had a broken leg, in addition to a troubled heart.

Much to my surprise, her leg was fine. Things were beginning to look up.

As I lifted the motorcycle off her, two of the men grabbed Nita and threw her into the back of their car before speeding off down the road. *They're stealing my wife!* My panicked brain chose the most media-worthy thought it could muster. I jumped onto my bike and started up the hill before noticing the third man standing by Nita's motorcycle waving and miming; he'd stay with her machine until I returned to pick it up. Got it. At the house, four women dressed in layered shirts, bright red scarves and ankle-length dresses greeted us with smiles and took Nita inside while I retrieved her bike and their stranded brother.

On my return, I found Nita in an unfinished cinder-block room, lying on a long, decorative bench that ran the length of the wall. She was being spoon-fed a meal of chicken stew, msemen (a dense Moroccan flatbread), honey, and homemade cookies. Next to Nita and tending her every need sat Fatma, a beautiful woman and the last of the sisters to be married. The three men who'd brought us here said their goodbyes and disappeared in a cloud of dust down the long dirt road, leaving us with the women and Bilay, the twenty-year-old nephew of Omar, the house-owner. Bilay spoke some French, but we had to communicate with the others using gestures and pantomime.

Fatma and Bilay weren't alone: his grandmother, three additional sisters, their two daughters, and a couple of young boys all lived together in that small home. Gathered in the hallway, everyone seemed to share an equal mix of concern and curiosity for their unexpected visitors. After an endless train of plates had made their way into the room, Nita began to fade into sleep, leaving plenty of awkward silences for me to fill. During one of these long and uncomfortable periods of quiet, Bilay suggested going for a walk in order to give Nita enough space to sleep. I could have used some rest myself, but seeing her eyes close and knowing she needed rest made me opt for the outdoors and a walk with my new friend.

As we scrambled up the steep path toward a wonderful outcropping of rock, I realized that *fields* of marijuana surrounded us. For a moment it stopped me in my tracks until Bilay's bright voice broke the silence. "Hashish! Hashish!" I looked up to see a wide grin on his face as he imitated drawing a long, deep drag from a joint. "All the green is marijuana." Nita and I had been taken in and given a home by some of the region's infamous hashish farmers.

* * *

For a long while, Bilay and I stare out from this slab of rock, our feet dangling over a valley filled with illicit drugs, watching the clouds devour the land. Somehow, it feels like an appropriate end to the past one hundred hours. Thinking of all of the potential outcomes manifesting in alternate universes fills my head with angst, but here, in this one, it's worked out well. We have shelter, we have food, and now we have new friends.

After what feels like hours, we make our way down to the house, past the family's pack of mangy-looking dogs, along a stone wall and in through the front door. Inside, Nita's awake and the smell of grilled goat and spice fills the air as food once again makes its way from some mysterious place to a plate in front of her. Fatma, who's now allowing Nita to feed herself, still looks quite concerned and hasn't left her side. We feel so grateful for this family and their endless hospitality.

The three men who found us on the roadside return and deliver a shopping bag filled with energy drinks to the table beside us. It's a kind gesture—though caffeine and sugar would push Nita's fragile heart over the edge. With a grateful smile, I take one and begin drinking it; I'm exhausted and I appreciate anything that will keep me awake for the evening. Bilay invites us for dinner (even though we haven't stopped eating since we arrived) and then ushers us down the hall to join the rest of his family for TV time.

Entering the living room, we're greeted by a mix of wide smiles, shy glances and curious stares. Nita wraps herself in a colourful blanket on a U-shaped bench and the relatives take their places around us, each with an excellent view of a small black and white television.

About halfway through what feels like a four-hour program, Nita suggests to me that she feels well enough to continue on tonight. It's a crazy thought, but I understand where it's coming from. We're in a house filled with strangers, our Canadian-ness makes us feel like we're imposing, and we're just over a hundred kilometres from our destination. A quick look at my watch puts the idea to rest; it's eight in the evening and though it's still light outside, the day will fade quickly in the mountains.

Besides, Nita and I are also beginning to fade. The toll of the day is making our eyes droop and there's little we can do to stop it. Dinner seems a long way away yet and, as we approach ten o'clock, we have to excuse ourselves from the room. We feel a little rude if I'm to be honest; I feel certain that they're making something special for us. I let Fatma know that I can come out again for dinner if she'd like, but Nita needs to sleep. Fatma doesn't seem upset, but a certain amazement is expressed at the possibility that we would consider missing dinner.

Our room promises much-needed peace and quiet. Fatma checks on us with Bilay and, after we assure her that we're doing well, she turns out the light and leaves. Like the end of any Peter Jackson movie, this false end to our night happens four or five more times. On the sixth entry we *promise* that we're fine and all that we need is rest. Fatma smiles, offers Nita some sweatpants and, with a graceful movement of hand from head to heart, leaves the room. A wonderful feeling of release rolls over us as we nestle into our sleeping bags and, in my fading thoughts, I believe sleep will soon follow.

It's at about this moment that the door flies open, dousing the room in a bright and unforgiving light.

"Kebabs!" beams Fatma, like a doting mum. Clearly, our plea for rest has fallen on deaf ears. Fatma and Bilay bring us each a plate of fantastic-smelling goat, spiced okra, and msemen, sitting with us at the table to make sure it all gets eaten. Even in a foggy, sleep-induced daze this food is some of the best we've tasted. Nita and I devour every scrap, both surprised at how hungry we are. Fatma, it seems, does know best.

Satisfied that we're well nourished, Fatma takes her leave and we succumb to the sleep that's eluded us all day.

It's *glorious.*

* * *

Nita and I wake early the following morning, joined only by Fatma, one of her sisters, and one of the young boys while we load our bikes under their careful supervision, refusing their repeated offers of breakfast. Nita's feeling better, but her heart remains too sensitive to risk any excitement, so we're setting off before any fuss can be made.

A golden light drenches the valley below as we say goodbye to our hosts. We offer a few euros for resupplying their cupboards, but they shoo our money away. Instead, Fatma gives us hugs, taps her heart with an open hand and smiles before stuffing our now-empty hands with another round of energy drinks for the day's journey.

We wave and, without waking the rest of the family, roll our bikes down the narrow gravel road.

At last, it seems, Morocco has let us in.

Issa Breibish embodies internationalism. He's a Canadian writer, adventure motorcyclist and world traveller of British and Libyan descent. He's spent two and a half years travelling the globe by motorcycle following a route that makes little sense to anyone else while supporting his non-profit organization, the Lost for Good Project (lostforgood. com). He's been chased by all manner of animal, detained as a spy in North Africa and has waited out a hurricane in the bowels of a ferry. He's not a spy but is an avid lover of coffee and great yarns spun around a campfire.

Web: WeLoveMotoGeo.com

Motorcycle Safari

Dom Giles

The following is an adaptation from the book Gone Riding. *Riding solo from Cape Town to Nairobi, Dom heads up the South African coast towards Swaziland on his BMW1200GS called Heidi.*

The small town of St. Lucia is surrounded by a UNESCO Natural World Heritage Site and is the most ecologically diverse tourist destination in Southern Africa. My guidebook told me I might see elephants, leopards, rhinos, buffalos, turtles nesting, crocs in the water, and hippos walking down the street. The area was famous for having the highest number of black rhino in one place, 525 species of birds, 35 species of frogs, 36 species of snakes, 800 hippos and 2,000 crocs. The tourist brochure said this: In 1928, Huberta, St. Lucia's most famous hippo, left her pod and began an epic journey of 1,600 kilometres across South Africa. In 1931, after crossing 122 rivers, she was killed by hunters in the Keiskamma River.

I had so many questions.

Keeping an eye out for Huberta's relatives crossing the road, I cruised into St. Lucia on Heidi hoping to find a campsite. (Heidi was my blue 2006 BMW1200GS that I had bought in Alaska. She had two Touratech panniers covered with stickers. I'd ridden her down to Panama and then shipped her over to South Africa. Somewhere along the way she told me her name was Heidi. We were now heading for Kenya.)

Unfortunately I couldn't see any signs, and as it was getting dark, I decided to check out a couple of the motels. I hadn't stayed in a motel yet in South Africa, and I was feeling a little lazy. Besides, I wanted to see what sort of value I would get for my money. I rode up the main street and as I came to the first motel, I saw the front wheel of a large motorcycle sticking out from behind a car in the parking lot. I pulled in to take a look.

Parked up next to one of the rooms was a yellow Suzuki V-Strom 650 with black metal panniers and a South African number plate. This was clearly the bike of a serious overlander—and a trusting one. It was after dark and he'd left several items just tied on with a bungee. However, there was no one around to talk to. Hoping that we would meet up later, I parked next to the V-Strom and went to the reception area. I had no idea what a nice room in a motel would cost in this part of the world, but I was confident it wouldn't be the $50 I'd had to pay in the USA. I was right. I got a nice clean room with a double bed, a fan and really hot water, all for $30. Camping would have probably cost me about $10, so now I knew I wouldn't break my budget by using motels every now and then.

After a quick wash and sort out, I went for a stroll around town. St. Lucia was certainly geared up for tourists, with a main street full of souvenir shops, restaurants, and tour guide offices. I found a pizzeria and ate while watching rugby on the large TV. This seemed to be the thing to do in South Africa and something I would just have to get used to. Food, beer and rugby—guess I couldn't complain. Eating out in the evening when I wasn't camping was often a lonely experience. Somehow, a person sitting alone in a restaurant (or even worse, sitting alone with a book) looks sad.

There's no rationale to this. They may well be very happy, and a good book beats bad company any day. Still, eating is a communal thing and it was often the one time of the day when I felt lonely.

When I got back to my room (there were no hippos about) I found a note on my bike. It read: "Alaska, we are in room 14. Leaving early in a.m. Want to do breakfast? Tom – Washington, Pat and Chris, Quebec." How could I refuse? I don't think I've ever done breakfast before.

What a surprise I got in the morning. "Tom – Washington" was the same Tom I'd met briefly, months before, at a motorcycle rally in Canada. He'd just bought the V-Strom in Johannesburg. Pat and Christianne were riding two-up on Pat's Canadian-registered Honda Africa Twin 750, which had been parked around the corner. The three had known each other for a few years and were planning to ride all the way up to Europe. We had a very long breakfast and swapped stories and pieces of advice for over three hours. Eventually they left, heading south, but we exchanged phone numbers and planned to head up to Namibia from Cape Town together. It looked as if my days of eating alone might be coming to an end … but not just yet.

From St. Lucia I headed north to my third African country, Swaziland. Like Lesotho, which I'd just been to, Swaziland was a country I'd heard of, could find on a map, but knew very little about. I knew it was landlocked and had gained independence from Britain in 1968. It was also one of the last remaining absolute monarchies in the world. King Mswati III, with a personal fortune of around $200 million, ruled over one of the poorest countries on the planet. Famous (or rather infamous) for his lavish lifestyle, this was the African king who had at least thirteen wives and held an annual dance where he could choose a new bride from among tens of thousands of bare-breasted virgins. Meanwhile, Swaziland had a horrific HIV/AIDS problem. The HIV infection rate was the highest in the world at about 26% of all adults, and over 50% of adults in their twenties. This had severely limited possible economic and social progress, and was at a point where it endangered the existence of its society as a whole. HIV had reduced life expectancy to below 50, and Swaziland could well become the first country in the world to actually collapse because of an epidemic.

With these thoughts banging around in my helmet, I left the border and entered Swaziland on a well-paved single-lane road. Even though I was only planning to be in the country for a few days, I was happy to pay the road tax if it meant all the roads were going to be as well maintained, sealed, and beautiful as the one I was on. The road swept up and over the hills and meandered alongside a river as I made my way northwards towards Mozambique. Just before the border, I reached the Mbuluzi Game Reserve that Tom and Pat had told me about. It didn't have any "dangerous" animals, so it allowed motorcycles. The thought of being able to ride in what was essentially a private game park and camp in the middle of it was too good an opportunity to miss. Tom had waxed lyrical about the place; they had seen giraffes and zebras and camped with monkeys and warthogs. I had to give it a go.

I turned up early in the afternoon, which was just as well as I wanted to get myself settled in the campsite with plenty of time to have a look around before sunset. I paid my $10 camping fee and rode through the reserve towards the campsite. The park ranger, who remembered Tom and Pat from the previous week, said I was the only camper and even though it was a Saturday they weren't expecting anyone else. I was going to have a Swaziland safari all to myself!

Tom had told me that they had seen giraffes on the way down to the campsite, but I didn't hold out much hope. I stood on my pegs as I rode the rough road down to the campsite, scanning the bush for any huge long-necked creatures just in case. I'd only been riding for about five minutes when I heard a noise off to my right and saw something rather large running parallel to me. The low African bushes suggested it wasn't a giraffe and as I glanced to my side I could just make out the distinctive black and white stripes of a zebra. I turned a corner, the bush opened out and I could see four or five zebras trotting along next to me, obviously spooked by the engine noise, but not overly concerned by my presence. I had to keep a careful eye on the road ahead because the compacted earth track was sandy in places, but I managed to keep looking over, amazed that I was riding along next to zebras.

Then I noticed something else out of the corner of my eye. I'd been concentrating so much on what was happening off to my right that I hadn't been paying attention to what was on my left. It took a double-take to realize what I was looking at: a huge animal lolloping along beside me, almost silently. I could hardly believe it was really a giraffe. And then there were three! To my right, half a dozen zebras were trotting through the bush, accompanying me, and to my left, three giraffes were also running alongside the bike. They were so huge and their strides so long it looked as if they were running in slow motion. I didn't know where to look or what to do. I just cruised along in second gear, easing off the throttle, trying to keep the bike upright as I glanced to my left and right in an effort to take it all in.

The whole thing only lasted a few seconds, but my heart was pumping and I had a huge smile on my face as the animals disappeared off into the bush and I continued down the track toward the campsite. I was indeed the only person camping and had the whole reserve to myself that night. I went for a two-hour walk (carefully avoiding the river as, apparently, it was home to crocodiles). When I got back to the campsite, I'd been joined by some monkeys and a family of warthogs. I don't know how far I was from the next human being, but I couldn't hear a single man-made noise or see any unnatural light. I was, to all intents and purposes, totally alone in the African bush; just me and Heidi on a Saturday night. It was dark by 6:30, but I didn't really care as I sat outside my tent under the bright stars of an African sky.

I felt calm, serene, untroubled by all the baggage that comes with modern life. I didn't care about anything or worry about anyone. It was a little epiphany similar, I imagine, to the kind of thing people can experience when they meditate. Briefly, in my own small way, my mind shifted a little onto a different plane. It wasn't consciously done, but I could feel the change.

I tried to hold on to that feeling of having achieved something, of peace and oneness with nature; the feeling that I was insignificant under the huge African sky, but that it didn't matter one bit. There had been times on the trip when I had felt lonely and missed company. But not that night; that night, company would have spoiled the experience. I needed to be alone—only then did it all, briefly, make sense.

*Dom Giles grew up in Jersey, a small island near France. After train-
ing to be a teacher, he spent the next twelve years working around
the world. He taught in Argentina, Colombia, Ethiopia, the Falkland
Islands, and Dubai. In 1995, he rode around Patagonia on a Honda
Transalp but it wasn't until 2010 that he'd saved enough money for
"the big one."*

*Dom had always wanted to visit Alaska and Namibia (he doesn't
like crowds!) and the rest of the route fell into place. Mainly on his
own, but accompanied by his wife for part of the trip, Dom explored
the wide-open spaces of North America, the steamy jungles of Central
America, and the life-affirming savannah of Southern Africa. He also
saved some turtles, cuddled some sloths, and taught poetry to some
South Africans.*

Web: DomGiles.co.uk
Twitter: @DomGiles1

The Great Question

Chris Becker

My left hand was numb. The heater in my left grip had stopped working and now the cold was starting to burn. I thought about placing my hand on the engine so the heat from its combustion process would warm it up, but I was afraid of letting go of the handlebars and losing control. I only dared to let go long enough to wipe the accumulated snow off my visor so I wouldn't be blind.

Not that I was seeing anything anyway. Only the two red brake lights, looking to me like the unblinking eyes of a demon staring at me out of a horrible whitemare, let me know that there was a car in front of me at all. I had lost all depth perception; those brake lights could have been fifty feet or five feet from me. A deluge of snow and ice obliterated everything else.

I was wearing a heated vest, but it only felt like someone had spilled a cup of hot coffee on my chest, leaving a small, burning, wet patch. The rest of me was just wet. And cold.

I became a small stone on a path that cars flowed around, and I envied their climate-controlled cockpits. Some of the cars had a window cracked, the heaters inside running too hot for the occupants. Deep within the bowels of my helmet, I sneered. Why not just run the AC? I thought bitterly. I tried to comfort myself with the knowledge that I was leaving the smallest carbon footprint possible. My fairly modest 800cc Suzuki gets about 45mpg, better than most hybrids. Some of the drivers who passed me looked at me, their faces frozen as they struggled to comprehend what their eyes saw. Their taillights disappeared into the storm like they were the eyes of phantasms, and I cursed their homes with rising acidic seas. As I sat there, shivering on my seat, my limbs forgotten extensions I could no longer feel, I became painfully aware of the limitations of riding a motorcycle in the Rockies.

This wasn't even winter. It was the last day of summer.

My only desire was to make it home without crashing. Somehow I found my exit. As I pried my hands from the handgrips and trudged through the door of my apartment, waiting for the inevitable pain when my fingers began to thaw, I asked myself The Great Question, the question I ask myself every time I come back from a ride drenched, frozen, and nearly hypothermic:

"Why do I ride?"

If once I had an answer, I had forgotten it now.

I have been riding a motorcycle for about ten years, starting with a scooter rental in Thailand, then a 1986 Kawasaki 454 and on up to my present bike, a 2008 Suzuki Boulevard.

If I am honest, I ask myself The Great Question more often than I don't.

A little illumination here: the Canadian Rockies is a picturesque and ideal riding environment. For about four months of the year. And a spotty four months at that. And your local weather report in the Rockies? It lies. On a motorcycle, it doesn't matter if ninety-five percent of the ride is a balmy ten degrees; you only have to get wet one time to ruin the enjoyment of the whole trip. Also, the design of my bike means that I am unable to adjust my riding position. Sure, it feels like a La-Z-Boy when I start out—my feet resting on the foot pegs like they were sprawled across my parents' coffee table—but after a few hundred kilometres with no way to move, my ass fat can no longer protect me. It's just too taut. (I think this is why there are so many fat guys on Gold Wings, the rich man's personal mobility scooter. They can go forever, their ass fat sustaining them when other, tauter, buttocks have failed. Someday in the future we will have flying harnesses for the portly gentleman like what the Baron Harkonnen uses in *Dune* but until then, Gold Wings. I have no idea how Ewan McGregor does it. Is he contributing to this book? "Ewan, how do you circumnavigate the world? We've all seen *Trainspotting*. You have no ass.") So, other than short, regional hops, the majority of motorcycle riding for me is an uncomfortable, even painful, experience. And safety? A motorcycle is safer than a car in many ways. It stops faster, accelerates faster, turns more sharply, and is smaller, making it much more nimble in avoiding an accident. However, if a rider ever finds him or herself in an accident, there is no crumple zone. The rider is the crumple zone. If I ever end up on the receiving end of the grill of a Ford F-350, my only hope is that I will have enough time to perform a Superman pose before travelling through its windshield.

And so: The Great Question. It seemed rhetorical to me, without an implied answer. Something to utter in exasperation: "What the hell? What is this shit?" (And, when I get distracted as I'm trying to write: "Damn internet!")

Moses found his answers in the desert, so I thought I would too. A few years back, I decided to make a trip down to Death Valley. If you ever want to experience the sensation of transitioning from hypothermia to heatstroke and back again, I recommend this trip highly. During the worst temperature extremes, the only way I could carry on was to congratulate myself on my choice of environmentally-friendly transportation. So that F-350's windshield I might be travelling through? It's an ecological disaster.

The route to Death Valley would take me through Montana, Utah, probably one or two other states, maybe Texas, according to a license plate I saw. The scenery was nice, but having come from the spectacle that was the Rocky Mountains, I found it a little underwhelming. This is the problem with living in a place that takes your breath away: it leaves just about any other natural wonder falling a little flat. So, although the ride was pleasant, after hundreds of kilometres my ass fat had long ago given way and the trip was now an exercise in endurance. By the time I hit Vegas, all I wanted to do was check in to my hotel room at Treasure Island and watch saucy pirates battle for control of the lobby on fake pirate ships. As I stood there, mesmerized by the dense symbolism of a ship of boy pirates boarding the girl pirate ship to plunder their "booty," I came to the sad realization that this could be the highlight of the entire trip. I meandered down the Strip, alone on an island of manufactured and tacky attractions, wondering if I should get rid of my motorcycle and stay close to home. Watch movies. Play video games.

With a heavy heart, I decided to cut my stay in Vegas a day short and head out into the desert. A wandering nomad deserves no more.

The next day, as I was packing, I felt a bit better after a solid night's sleep, but still generally disappointed with the whole trip. "What was this about, anyway?" I asked myself as I went over the rest of my travel plans. I checked out, collected my bike from the garage and headed out. The locals had been complaining about the heat, so I knew it was hot already, but I wasn't prepared for what I was about to experience. I won't bore you, dear reader, with numbers, but I will say it was hot enough to make me sweat like a loaf of Spam. I hoped that when I achieved highway speed I would begin to cool down, but navigating through the city was excruciating. Not to mention I am a Canadian. This meant that not only was I not acclimatized to the ferocious temperature, but I was also wearing a full-face helmet and heavy leathers because, you know, the weather could change any minute and an ice storm blow in.

As I left the city and headed west, the rushing air felt more like a hair dryer than a soothing fan, but eventually the sun achieved its apex and began to fall. I had figured that I would just be entering Death Valley National Park right around dusk and this would at least take the edge off the desert heat, making it somewhat pleasant to ride in. I couldn't have been more wrong. The heat was crushing, merciless and omnipresent. There was no reprieve. The sun had sunk below the distant mountains, and yet the air seemed to be on fire. I tried alleviating some of the heat by lifting my visor. Have you ever had cookies in the oven and wanted to take a quick look inside to see how they were doing, so you opened the oven, only to be met with a wall of heat that made your eyes water? Same thing. Except, not only did my eyes water because of the heat, they were also the cookies. They became inflamed like a baking sheet of oatmeal chocolate chips. I slammed my visor shut again. "Why is it so hot?! Where is it coming from? There is literally no sun! There needs to be a sun for it to be this hot! I am figuratively melting! This can't be possible!" Beside me passed a car with a family in it, the AC obviously cranked. The children were laughing; I assumed at me. I glared at them. "You. You are why the polar ice caps are melting. Do you have any idea how much energy you are using having the air conditioner on like that!? And look at how much space is in that vehicle! You could fit twenty people in there! Way to destroy the Earth! My motorcycle gets like a thousand miles to the gallon! I AM CAPTAIN PLANET!" At that moment I didn't just ride a Suzuki. I was *David Suzuki.*

By the time I had reached the park, I was drained and the shadows were beginning to lengthen as the sun made its final plunge. I started to gain elevation as I rode, the light from the setting sun mixing in with the red desert rock, giving the landscape an unearthly hue. The road began to twist as I climbed, and I wondered when I would actually see Death Valley, the lowest piece of dry land in North America. The Great Question was always in the back of my mind.

And then the valley opened up. It was empty. Gloriously empty. I could see the other side, but barely. To my left and right, the desert below me vanished into the horizon. It was magnificent. For a few precious moments, I forgot all about the insufferable heat and looked down into what I imagine oblivion must look like. Nothingness. Like the Montana sky or a frozen ocean. The Rockies is spectacular in a different way, a way that encapsulates the bounty of God. This was the opposite. Almost terrifying. It was as if this was His wrath; endless, burning, remorseless. But no less glorious. I took all the sensations in and locked them away into a part of my soul. The heat, wind, smell, vision—all became a part of who I was at that very moment. The road undulated as I rode, as if I was travelling down the skeletonized remains of a dragon cast out of Heaven, the impact of its planet-fall creating the desert before me. And I said to myself, as if it was part of some ancient, forgotten liturgy that I had unearthed in the ruins of a crumbling church: "This is why I ride." I took a breath of super-heated air and then plunged myself into the fiery, wonderful abyss.

Hallelujah.

Chris Becker is a moron who spurned his editor's many requests to provide a biography, thus unwisely forcing said editor to write the biography himself. Although Becker technically can ride a motorcycle, he cannot do it well. He lives in Banff, Alberta, which he seems rather proud of for no good reason. For the past ten years, he has been trying to finish a short novel. If it ever comes out, it will be a miracle. But it might also be good. It's called God and Zeros. *Look for it in the incredibly distant future.*

High on the Plateau

Carl Parker

Mark Twain once said, "There comes a time in every rightly constructed boy's life when he has a raging desire to go somewhere and dig for hidden treasure." And so it was I found myself a young man teaching business English in Chengdu, the capital of Sichuan, the Chinese province neighbouring Tibet. When you're young and unfettered, teaching is a great way to travel the world, do fulfilling and interesting work, and still have spare time for a few misadventures.

Having just ridden a 1997 Bandit 1200S around the United States and Canada a few months prior, I was anxious to travel and live in China, but had no idea if owning a vehicle there was even possible. Charles Poynton, a fellow university teacher and Australian geologist, had been bumming around the world on various forms of personal transportation for years. It was pure good fortune we met shortly after my arrival in China. When he offered up a holiday drive into the nearby mountains of eastern cultural Tibet, I couldn't turn him down.

Before I realized it, we'd ascended a visually stunning, barren, rocky pass over 4,000 metres high. My face was pressed against the fogged-up window of Charles' 1000cc microvan, sometimes called a "bread loaf van" in Chinese. Having only ridden in North America where the bikes are relatively large, I was surprised to see so many small motorcycles all over the mountain roads. Even in these high and desolate areas, they often shuttle locals and supplies between towns and isolated villages year-round, in all kinds of weather. Couples also toured the mountains of Tibet on tiny overloaded 125cc scooters, making me re-think the role of small bikes in the global motorcycling community.

Unless travelling over a pass in Tibet, roads usually followed rivers or meandered through grasslands or high-altitude deserts. Fortunately, Charles enjoyed stopping for scenic breaks, often near 700-year-old Tibetan stone houses built into the mountainsides. Many had towers which once were lit as part of a simple warning system during invasions. At one such stop, the local mayor pulled up on a 150cc cruiser just to say hello and ask if we needed assistance. After the usual "Where you coming from, where you going?" conversation, he noticed my interest in his bike and asked if I'd like to take it for a spin.

Without hesitation, my ass found the saddle as if by magnetic force. The bike was similar to a Virago 250, sported a bent handlebar, and lacked working gauges. The engine sounded and felt like a sewing machine that wanted to stall at idle. Despite all this, and the bike's wooden brakes, it was one of the happiest moments I've ever had on a motorcycle. The river road was all curves, which drew me farther than I probably should have allowed it to, until the bike inevitably stalled and had to be push-started. The owner likely assumed I was just going to take his bike up the road a bit—not for a joy ride. Returning late, I thanked him with a huge grin. But I now had an idea brewing that riding a bike in China might be possible. Maybe more importantly, it established in me a commitment to exploring western China—in all its sheer massiveness, the good, bad, and ugly—by small motorbike. I would do whatever it took to make that happen, and it would be worth it. For a budding adventurer, this is one of the earliest and most crucial challenges to overcome.

Although getting a license as a foreigner took great effort, most everything else was wonderfully inexpensive and easy. Second-hand bikes were sold with license plates, and registration documents were generally passed on with the vehicle purchase. All one really had to do was have the correct personal travel paperwork and make sure the bike ran.

For those who like to tinker, China is a wrench-spinner's paradise. Small Chinese bikes are simple to work on in "shade-tree mechanic" fashion. The markets are full of small shops packed with specialized parts. If you want something replaced, repaired or customized, you simply install and test it before purchasing. I found that a set of longer forks or shocks, for example, could be purchased for about $60. Another shop might sell just engine parts. Want a pumper carb? No problem, that'll be 30 bucks and about 30 minutes for installation.

Just because parts were available everywhere didn't necessarily mean you got them at the best prices. Many shops had unscrupulous owners who were more than willing to give a "special foreigner discount" of 300% more than a local would pay. Before too long, I figured out the real rates, along with the dance required to get a fair price. It's well worth learning the fine art of haggling, and China is a great place to do it. Moreover, it's a handy skill for more than just buying motorbike parts.

In the spring of 2008, Beijing and the rest of China were preparing for the Summer Olympics spectacular. Domestic issues made travelling on the Tibetan plateau problematic but Lorne Smith, a Guangdong-based American expat, and I went on a little adventure ride southwest of

Chengdu towards Yunnan and western Sichuan, which was once again mostly ethnic Tibetan. One town we stopped at had only very basic "*bing guan*" (motels). Picking a place when you're not camping can be a gamble, but you eventually learn how to spot shady staff or owners who often present themselves in all sorts of costumes, including posing as monks. We weren't too sure about the place we selected, but when it's raining and you're wet, just getting warm and dry takes priority.

With bare walls and no western toilet, the place wasn't ideal, but at least the bikes were safe and the beds lacked stains or dried drool on the pillows. Hot water was largely unavailable and the windows didn't have screens, which meant either a sticky night in a stuffy room or providing a buffet for the town mosquitoes. The owner was a nice guy, but his wife ran the show and was a stickler for price. She wouldn't budge from 80 RMB, easily twice the going rate. (A note to future China motorcycle travellers, if you ever try to bargain for a room do NOT bring your bike or bags into the hotel before the deal is struck—otherwise they'll think they've got you. And if it's raining, they probably do.)

We noticed the lack of a few amenities, so in a playful manner decided to ask for some, since we were paying a premium. The husband was taking care of chores in the courtyard parking area and presented a good opportunity. The ensuing conversation went something like this:

"Excuse me, our room has no towels."

"No towels? Oh … well … we don't put towels in our rooms."

"For 80 RMB you don't provide towels?" I said with a smile.

He scratched his head and passing the buck, said "Okay, I'll ask my wife."

A few moments later she appeared. "You want towels? We don't use towels."

"Then how do you shower?"

"We use very small hand towels." This was actually common. If they really didn't have any towels, I normally used a dry shirt, but this had now become an exercise of wits, so I replied "Hand towels are okay."

"Oh, these are just the small towels we use ourselves," she said hoping to imply they are not suitable for guests.

"That's fine, we don't need special towels."

She eventually left and returned with one small, scratchy, and heavily-used hand towel barely capable of soaking up anything.

"But there are two of us!"

"We only have one!" she said, walking off.

It may seem like a lot of hassle for such a small reward, but this kind of interaction is common in China, and more often than not results in making new friends. Cigarettes are also commonly passed out in the middle of a good negotiation, making haggling a chance to understand each other through the battle of commerce wills. If you can haggle well, it's fun, it will save a few bucks, and you may even find it earns a little respect. Giving and commanding respect is important as a traveller. You neither want to be taken advantage of nor appear disrespectful when you can only rely on body language for communication.

I met riders throughout China who were obsessed with planning. Everything had to go as planned—even the slightest mishap would be cause for great, childish tantrums. I found the best time was had by riders with open and dynamic mindsets who found something to appreciate in any encounter. Rigidity in the soul only makes the journey unpleasant for others, and possibly dangerous for the rider. No matter how cheap or expensive your bike is, it will break down eventually and you'll need help. Having a confident but honest and respectful demeanour will go much farther on the Tibetan plateau, and in many areas of life.

The astonishing cultural and geological allure of Tibet needs to be experienced to be fully understood. Big mountains (averaging 4,500 metres high) give way only to bigger mountains which dominate the horizon. At nearly every pass, I could look west and see a dangerous-looking skyline of hard, sharp, and dark snow-capped crags jutting powerfully into deep blue skies vividly spotted with thick white clouds.

Tibetan pastoral life in the high-altitude grasslands is harsh, but fosters an earnest and warm appreciation for other people. Nomads still live a lifestyle largely dependent upon yaks for food, fuel, shelter, and even art materials. Nothing is wasted and every encounter with a new person is something to look forward to. Crowded cities can make for unwanted neighbours, but living in a vast expanse of wilderness means people are important for news, support, and simply having fun passing time. Solitude can be bliss, but good companionship is heavenly wherever you are, even if only for a short while. The most generous are often those with the least to give, and this philosophical dichotomy is both logically confounding and at the heart of what it means to be a good person. Though time together may be brief, chance encounters in the wilderness may be life-changing and cause for quiet gratitude and reflection.

In contrast, some parts of Tibet are less friendly. There, the judicious use of good manners can make the difference between getting home safely and disappearing in the middle of nowhere. Tibet proper used to be divided into the Tibetan, Kham and Amdo regions. The Amdo region is now mostly what's called the Qinghai province, which borders the Gobi and Taklimakan deserts to the north. Both deserts were the eastern terminus of the Silk Road and hotbeds for power struggles lasting hundreds or thousands of years. Amdo Tibetans are known for being a little more warlike, perhaps by necessity.

Riding through Qinghai, I could tell the demeanour had changed from the more happy-go-lucky nomads to surly-looking horse or motorcycle riders with sun-wrinkled hands, thick wool robes, large knives, heavy leather boots, and cowboy hats. They would commonly purchase supplies in old, small, general stores, where their hard heels would resonate on the wooden plank floorboards, making the scene feel much like the old American Wild West. Add in some hairy eyeballs, and a solo rider may unavoidably end up in an "uncomfortable" situation. Knowing your fate has been, and always will be, in the hands of others to a certain degree brings a new appreciation for keeping a respectful attitude. Knowing when to press a matter and when to back off may save you from grave danger.

I did encounter a few negative situations encountered in five years of motorbiking western China, but the overwhelming majority of my experiences there were bridge-building and life-affirming—even if perplexing at times. While the landscapes were physically amazing, what ultimately mattered were the lessons about humanity that continually added to my understanding of the personal potential and the fraternal nature of mankind. Regardless of age or era, nothing can replace the new perspectives on life which come from embracing an adventurous spirit.

Life is inherently full of adventure if we make it so. Some of us are adventurers and don't even know it. Riding around the world, just as with starting a family or a business, is a monumental effort we willingly undertake despite the risks and sacrifices. For some, risk is an excuse not to play; for others it's the challenge to overcome through questioning what we value in life, and to choose how to spend our most precious and ever-expiring resource—time. What will we do today, and how will it matter?

After completing his first feature-length film, The Return: Riding Western China (available at ADVMotoShop.com), Carl came away from five amazing years of photographing western China with two important lessons. First, the rider makes the ride—not the other way around. Second, sharing your journey with others expands not only your personal horizons, but the horizons of those around you as well. Carl founded MyChinaMoto.com, a forum dedicated to riding in China, and currently publishes Adventure Motorcycle (ADVMoto) *magazine.*

Web: AdventureMotorcycle.com

The Cedars of God

Jeremy Kroeker

The following is an adaptation from the book Through Dust and Darkness, *published by Rocky Mountain Books (RMBooks.com). Used with permission.*

I poked at the neutral switch until the green light flickered on. The engine didn't want to start at first, but it finally sputtered to life. After that it rose in pitch to a healthy idle. The exhaust came in metered bursts, making the leaves jump on a nearby bush. In the cool air you could see the smoke. As the bike warmed up, I looked it over.

The odometer on the old KLR 650 showed 40,000 kilometres. I had put most of them on the machine, but I think a former owner tampered with the odometer and lied about the mileage when he sold it to me. The bike was getting tired. It had a mysterious wobble in the front end, so I called it The Oscillator. Still, it had taken me this far and I had grown to trust it.

I had flown the bike from Canada to Germany. From there I rode it through the Balkans, then through Greece, Turkey and Syria. Now it was parked outside a dank hotel in Beirut, Lebanon, just opposite a building dating back to the French Mandate, all spackled with bullet holes from the civil war.

After all those miles, I hadn't ridden the bike much lately. There were restrictions on motorcycles south of Beirut. Years ago, armed men on little scooters committed murder in Sidon and, overreacting as only Lebanese politicians can, the government banned all motorcycles from the city and on the main highway going south. So I chained the bike to a fence outside the hotel and took day trips with public transport.

"I know I've been ignoring you," I whispered, patting the gas tank, "and I'm sorry." I strapped up my helmet, still talking softly to the machine. "You know. It's just easier to take a taxi with all those blockades."

If The Oscillator resented the neglect, it didn't show. Together we rode north, toward Tripoli. Nearing the city, I turned away from the coast and climbed into the hills toward a low bank of cloud. When I stopped at the edge of a town to check my map, an old man waved me over to join him for coffee on his porch. Bundled up against a chill in the mountain air, he wore a long woollen jacket and a black hat. We took turns leafing through my Arabic phrasebook in an effort to communicate, but that only frustrated us both. In the end we sat quietly, enjoying the cool air and hot coffee.

One side of the man's porch nudged the road, while the other side opened onto a rocky yard. From there, the property fell away into the holy ground of the Qadisha Valley. The valley is home to several Christian monasteries and the town of Bcharre.

Crags in this valley often split open into caves, and these caves have for centuries attracted hermits aspiring to religious perfection. Whether any have attained it or not, who can say? But you have to admire their resolve.

Looking across the gap, I could see a village of white houses perched at the far edge of grey cliffs. Hardy green shrubs clung to the rock down low, while farther upslope the leaves had gone yellow. Higher still, a dusting of snow settled on grey mountaintops. Above that, there was thick grey cloud.

Way down below, the Qadisha River ran through the valley. Its headwaters are in a grotto very near The Cedars of God. That was my destination: the last remaining grove of Lebanon's ancient cedars.

The road wound through villages with red roofs and Christian symbols, through Bcharre, past a domed church with two towers and farther up toward the Cedars. Parking the bike, I slid out of the saddle to stand on numb feet. I swung my arms to warm the blood in my fingers. As my joints had grown stiff from the cold, I took several testing steps before picking up the pace. Walking down, I passed through an opening in a stone fence and entered the forest. Technically it was closed for the season, but that only meant that I had the place all to myself.

My footsteps made no sound: the path lay beneath a blanket of needles and seed cones that had fallen from the trees. Patches of snow gathered in shady hollows. The cedars were anchored to the earth with their wide bases, their thick boughs stretched out like giants flexing for show.

A cold rain fell as I padded along. It washed the scent of cedar right out of the air. Water trickled off my head along ringlets of hair, pausing at the tips before dropping away in front of my eyes.

I looked around for signs of life. I listened. Nothing but the plunking of rain off my shoulders. I wished that I could share the moment with someone, that I had someone to talk to. A few times I even caught myself speaking out loud, talking to the trees—or maybe I was just talking to myself. Either way, the trees remained silent.

The Cedars. Even with all the majesty that remained, they only hinted at a former glory. Once a wild forest, the cedars are now confined to several national parks. All the trees in this reserve had been pruned, their limbs sawn off, their stumps painted to protect them from disease. The almighty cedars. Humans built walls around them. Men placed them in a box to define their boundaries. Men trimmed them and made them into something less wild.

Returning to the bike, I wiped the seat with the back of my glove to clear away the water. The map showed a track that crossed over the mountains before dropping down into the Beqaa Valley. I looked up into the hills. Heavy fog had settled over the peaks, making it impossible to see. But as I looked at the map, that route appealed to me.

I idled up to the only tourist shop still open this late in the season. I asked the girl behind the counter about the path. Was it open? Was it a good road?

The girl was unaccustomed to fielding questions like this in English. She could really only talk about the price of her curios. But after searching for the words, she did manage to articulate a warning. "There is snow," she said. "It's too difficult for him." She meant The Oscillator. "He'll fall."

I decided to ride up anyway and take a look for myself. I've ridden in the snow before and I was imagining the dry, powdery stuff I had seen lower in the valley.

With a wave to the girl, I rode into the fog. I'll bet she could still hear my engine when heavy snow forced me to turn around. As the road pushed through the clouds, it entered a landscape of slush. I pressed on, thinking that I might be near the crest of the pass. But the sleet that stuck to my visor provided no traction for my tires. The Oscillator very nearly did fall. When I stopped in the middle of the road to warm my hands, I couldn't get moving again. The back tire just spun and spun. Defeated, I executed a fifteen-point turnaround to retreat, then, dragging both feet, I slipped back down the mountain until the sleet became cold rain once again. As I rode past the tourist shop, I looked for the girl. She was gone.

When I had left Beirut that morning, I had brought along a small backpack with the intention of staying in a new town for the night; but now, too tired, too wet to bother finding a hostel, I settled in for a miserable ride in the dark and rain all the way back to Beirut.

Jeremy Kroeker is the author of Motorcycle Therapy *and* Through Dust and Darkness.

Web: MotorcycleTherapy.com
Twitter: @Jeremy_Kroeker

Missed a Date with the Sausage Creature

Andreas Schroeder

At 6:30 am on July 14, 2009, I stepped out of my motel room in Merritt, B.C. into a quiet, still slightly chilly day. The sun was already up and I knew that by noon it was going to be a scorcher, but for now the air was crisp and the birds were flitting about enthusiastically. I thought about having breakfast at a family restaurant just up the highway, but the coolness of the morning was too valuable to waste. I wiped the dew off my windshield, pulled on my helmet and armoured jacket, and fired up the bike. Then I rolled it to the far end of the parking lot to warm it up.

I had fuelled up the night before, and checked all my running gear, so I was ready to roll. There was no traffic on Merritt's main street, and no cars yet at the cement foundry on the northwestern edge of town. I cruised slowly through the Lower Nicola Indian reservation several kilometres farther west, and then let fly onto Highway #8 into the Nicola Valley, along the river. The air was tangy with oxygen, the pavement near-new and dry, and the river sparkled as it foamed over rocks. The bike was performing flawlessly, my reflexes were feeling sharp and reliable, and as I cranked my speedometer past 120 kilometres per hour, swooping through curve after curve, I felt wonderfully alive.

The Nicola Valley is a true valley, but in places it's more like a canyon.

There are sections where its walls move in so close to the highway that, blasting through, you feel as if your shoulders might almost scrape rock. Most corners in those sections are blind, and your only hint of what's ahead are the speed signs. But "Slow to 30" at a curve entrance can signal anything from a merely tight corner, to a decreasing-radius curve, to a sequence of blind S-bends, to a stretch of dangerously broken pavement. It means, at the very least, that when you round that curve, you might encounter a bigger challenge than what you can readily see just as you're entering it.

Nevertheless, the last thing I expected at 7 o'clock in the morning was an oncoming, fully loaded logging truck.

I saw the top of his radiator rise into view above the curve before I saw anything else—but that told me everything I didn't want to know. At five car-lengths long, he had to be cutting diagonally across the corner I was just entering. And at the speed I was travelling, I needed every bit of my lane to get through that corner myself.

There was no time to brake—and no point in braking anyway. Abruptly braking a motorcycle in a situation like this would just have compounded the problem.

There was really only one thing to do—lean the bike even harder into the corner, to decrease the radius of my turn to the absolute max.

Easier said than done—my VTX had a low centre of gravity and limited ground clearance. If I leaned any more, I risked dragging its floorboard on the pavement; if a floorboard hits a pothole and digs in, it can spin a bike out of control so fast, it's more like an explosion.

This all raced through my head in a split second, but went nowhere. There was no other option anyway. I gripped the handlebars as rigidly as

I could, forced the bike over until my right thigh could almost feel the rushing pavement, and hung on.

There was an angry scream of grinding metal as a long rooster-tail of sparks arced out from under my right floorboard. Was I down? I had to be running virtually on my tires' sidewalls at this angle. For a nano-second, the problem became more psychological than mechanical: every cell in my body was shouting at me that this sound was wrong, wrong, desperately wrong. Do something different!

The truck was already almost on top of me, towering several storeys high; no way to tell whether my trajectory was going to run me right under its wheels. I knew if I tried making any further adjustments it would all be over in an instant, but I also felt, with an equal conviction, that it was over anyway. My orbit was sweeping me toward the truck's wheels with heart-stopping speed.

Then: a burst of darkness, a stunning detonation of air, the stupefying roar of diesel engine and wheel howl, and a vicious spray of road sand, bark chips and tree sap. I felt my rear tire slam into something rock-hard, presumably one of the truck's wheels, a jolt that passed with tremendous force through the bike's frame right up into my fingertips—and then the dark abruptly vanished and I was back in the sun, the truck behind me, my floorboard still spraying sparks and the bike now headed straight for the canyon wall.

When knocked off your trajectory on a motorcycle, the biggest danger is over-correction—the tendency to base adjustments on fear rather than math. It was the second time in as many seconds that I had to ignore one voice to follow another: Not as much as you think, damn it! Not that much! Not even *that* much!

The bike was back up but now fish-tailing, tires screeching. It twisted and lurched. I struggled to keep the corrections small, but I just couldn't stop the bucking. Some imperative other than my own was determining the bike's behaviour. Then somehow, in that mad melee, one particular jack pine among the thousands growing up the side of the canyon wall swam into my view and sharpened into focus. I saw it, registered it, and locked on. Forced myself to stay connected to that tree. Made it the only thing that mattered.

Almost instantly the bucking changed—or maybe it merely stopped registering. Everything became reduced to me seeing that tree, and the fierce straight line between us. I felt the motorcycle become irrelevant; it was now just something struggling beneath me on the way to that tree. In this rearrangement of priorities, the struggling abruptly subsided and the bike straightened into line. I was back in control.

I rolled back the throttle, shifted out of gear, and pulled onto a level stretch of shoulder. My fingers were trembling so badly, I couldn't get a proper grip on the ignition key. Finally I just balled up my fist and hit the kill switch.

The engine died.

In the sudden silence, laced with either the singing of cicadas or the hissing of the blood through my brain, I could still hear the rumble of the logging truck in the distance, growling his way through another corner.

That's when I registered the one sound I hadn't heard as our trajectories had merged: the hiss of his air brakes, or at least the snarl of his Jake brake. Something to indicate he'd pulled his foot off his gas pedal at that critical moment.

He hadn't. The sonofabitch had just bombed through. As if he hadn't seen me at all.

And then I realized that he very likely hadn't. Because that curve hadn't merely been tight, but also humped in the middle. His cab would have been rising as he entered it, his windshield aimed at the sky. And I'd been leaning over so hard, I'd probably been far below his vision.

I listened some more. I could still hear him, miles down the valley, his diesel's growl snorting intermittently as he worked the gears. Totally oblivious. Totally focused on getting that rig down to one of the sawmills I'd passed less than half an hour before. Totally unaware of the momentous thing that had just happened to us.

I couldn't decide whether to laugh or to be pissed off.

I stayed there on that shoulder for another fifteen minutes or so. Motionless. Now and then a pickup passed by. Nobody paid any attention to me.

When the trembling finally stopped, I straightened up, toggled back on the kill switch, fired up, and took off down the road.

I thought I might drive more slowly for a while.

I was definitely willing to do that.

It seemed only respectful, somehow.

But within ten minutes I was back up to speed, back in the groove, fully engaged with the bike and the road.

Running as fast as I'd been running before.

Andreas Schroeder has been both a motorcyclist and a writer for roughly 50 years. During that time he's owned at least a dozen motor-cycles—mostly cruisers and tourers—and published some 20 books, including nonfiction, fiction, poetry and journalism. He currently rides a Honda ST1300 and holds the Rogers Communications Chair in Creative Nonfiction at UBC's School of Creative Writing. He lives with his wife Sharon Brown in Roberts Creek on BC's Sunshine Coast.

Web: apschroeder.com

Ladakh and Zanskar

Geoff Hill

"The Himalayas are still growing, and at the same time collapsing, possibly overnight and across our route."
   Blazing Trails website

I normally phone out for curry on a Sunday night, but the other week I thought I'd pop out for a change.

Lovely little place, and you can't miss it. Just fly to Delhi, take a domestic flight to Leh in the Himalayas, walk up the main street, past the Tibetan refugees selling prayer wheels, several holy cows, and VJ Singh's Refrigartor (*sic*) Repairs, and the Ibex Restaurant is next on the left, past the Leh Super Shopee (also *sic*).

I recommend the Chicken Tandoori.

It was no ordinary night out, but then this was no ordinary trip: two weeks riding 1,000 miles of the wildest and highest roads in the world, 400 of those on dirt tracks made of sand, mud, gravel, rocks, rivers and, in one memorable case, snow.

Still, at least I knew who to blame: Peter Stilwell, who was sitting next to me tucking into a Rogan Josh washed down by a bottle of Kingfisher.

A 26-year-old biology researcher from Totnes in Devon, he'd travelled in India before, and back home bought one of the Royal Enfields which have been made in Madras since the British company set up a satellite factory there in 1949 to make them for the Indian Army.

The British factory closed in 1970, but today Madras is still turning out 100,000 brand-new vintage Enfields a year, and Peter saw the chance to combine his two loves when he insured his bike with Bennetts and discovered the company ran a competition called Bennetts Biking Dreams, a sort of "Jim'll Fix It" for bikers to write in and describe their ultimate biking adventure in the hope of winning it.

The next thing he knew, he and his childhood mate and fellow biker Vince Stephens were on a flight to Delhi, and I was with them to keep an eye on them over two weeks with Blazing Trails, the bike adventure company of Suzie Lumsden and her husband Damon l'Anson, which organizes group tours in India, Nepal and soon South Africa, and who Bennetts had chosen to make Peter's dream a reality.

"It's been quite surreal, really. It only began to feel real when we got on the plane to Delhi and then on to Ladakh," said Peter as we decamped at Leh, the breathtaking starting point for the toughest and most remote of Blazing Trail's trips.

And it's not breathtaking just because of the seething mass of soldiers, refugees, carpet salesmen, pashmina traders, trinket hawkers, sacred cows, less sacred donkeys, and more sacred monks.

And it's not just because of wandering around the streets trying to take in the seething mass of soldiers, refugees, carpet salesman, pashmina traders, trinket hawkers, sacred cows, less sacred donkeys and more sacred monks, all to the background sound of India: the slow heartbeat of single-cylinder Enfields coming and going with up to four people on board.

No, it's also because at over 10,000 feet, the moment you step off the plane, you're all set for the headaches, giddiness, and altitude sickness which Blazing Trails thankfully gives you a day to get over.

After that, every ride on an Enfield starts with a small but important lesson in how to start it, for although the newest UK imports come with a new-fangled electric start, Blazing Trails uses lovingly-maintained examples of the older models, which need to be kicked carefully into life. This process involves either your ankle turning blue with bruises, and the air around you likewise with cursing and swearing, or a smug grin as the 500cc single phuts softly into life.

Not only do the bikes have kick-start, but their four-speed gearboxes are on the right in the old British style, resulting in much hilarity for the first few miles as several of our group of eight tried to brake and found themselves causing grievous bodily harm to the gears, accompanied by looks of weary horror from the group's accompanying mechanics, Jamal and Ramji.

Still, at least the planned first day was a gentle 90-mile introduction on tarmac, giving us a chance to get used to the bikes as we tootled along merrily making extensive use of the most important button on any vehicle in India—the horn.

Heavens, it was all so civilized that Peter was even wearing a well-pressed white shirt with cufflinks, since a chap has to set an example in the Raj.

In fact, I can safely say that all was going swimmingly until our first stop at a roadside shack for a refreshing cup of chai, the hot, sweet, milky tea that soon becomes addictive in India.

"Mmm. Bit suspicious that there's no traffic coming the other way," said our outrider, Adam Lewis, a superbly skilled biker who was just taking a break from an around-the-world journey which started in 2006 and shows no signs of ending.

His suspicions were right: discreet enquiries in the direction of the proprietor elicited the news that a landslide had blocked the way ahead, and a team was trying to dynamite it clear.

We ordered more chai, and settled into that state of Buddhist acceptance which comes from things moving inexorably outside your control.

On the wall, a flyer for the Gentle Man Tailors barely stirred in the listless heat, above a baffled Spanish family and a pair of Japanese hippy chicks.

After two hours, Suzie had had enough.

"I know a short-cut. Let's go," she said, leading us back up the road and along hours of mountainous farm track. Steep hairpin bends of sand and rock with optimistic tractors coming the other way, that sort of thing.

We stopped briefly in a verdant valley for chai beside a cow meadow and a gurgling stream, and finally, as the sun sank behind the snowy peaks, we rolled into the courtyard of a little hotel in the mountain retreat of Lamayuru, in the shadow of a 1,000-year-old monastery which is home to 150 monks, some of whom looked as if they had been there from day one.

The showers were cold, the beer was colder, and the curry for dinner was hot, but we were so tired we couldn't have cared less which order they came in.

The next day, we seemed to pass another Indian Army barracks every few miles. The country spends an estimated £4 million a week guarding these northern regions, which have been disputed by Pakistan ever since Partition in 1947, and which are now even more disputed with the brooding presence of China in Tibet to the northeast.

They'd be better spending it on the roads, I thought grimly as we bounced west along a route to Kargil on which stretches of decent road would tempt us coyly for a couple of miles, then disappear yet again into a boulevard of broken dreams.

And yet, just as my heart sank at rounding a corner to see yet another stretch of sand, gravel or mud, it would lift at the sight of a lush valley bright with wild roses, or a group of children waiting for a school bus, their uniforms immaculate, or once, a beautiful Buddhist nun spinning a prayer wheel.

Even to gaze upon her face was like a meditation to me.

By the afternoon, we were in the verdant Suru River valley, home to bears, wolves, and snow leopards (one of which walked into a village near here some years ago and lay down in the street, to die three days later in spite of the locals' gifts of milk and food).

"Here," I said to Damon at the next chai stop, "how long does this crap road go on for?"

"All the way to Padum tomorrow, and then the same all the way back. And it gets worse," he grinned.

"Tell you what. I'll ask Ramji [the assistant mechanic] if he fancies a spin on my bike, and I'll jump in the backup truck for a bit," I grinned back.

It was the right decision. Freed from constantly looking a few yards past the front wheel, I got the chance to look out of the window at stunning views and wave cheerily at road workers camped in makeshift tents, grazing yaks, and plump marmots.

One even sat by the roadside, completely unconcerned as I walked over, then, having decided I wasn't a golden eagle who was going to eat him for afternoon tea, waddled off to sit on a nearby rock and keep a lookout for raiding Pakistani marmots.

Peter, meanwhile, had been so traumatized by the road that he had not only abandoned his cufflinks, but was sporting a shirt with at least two creases in it.

Shocking. No wonder we lost the Empire.

"Spectacular. Great ride. Knackered," was his verdict on the day as he climbed off, covered in dust, at the campsite in the shadow of Rangdum, a monastery hamlet looking out over a valley which would have been a worthy setting for *The Lord of the Rings*.

In the morning, we wound our way up another high pass, gazed down in wonder at the vast Darang Durung glacier, then wound our way down at length through the Zanskar Valley.

Its villages and hamlets, from the faces and clothing of the inhabitants to the Buddhist shrines, were pure Tibetan, yet the surrounding landscape, with its dry stone walls, grassy fields, willow and poplar groves, bubbling streams, and white houses with thatched roofs, was disturbingly Irish.

It was all very confusing, so the only answer was to stop for the night at Padum, an end-of-the-road town with a frontier feel to its dusty streets.

After a tour of the highlights, which took about 45 seconds, we went on a pub crawl (to both of them), then decamped to what the guidebook described as "the least worst restaurant in town."

Sadly, the Afghani Chicken was off, presumably having gone off to fight a US Army chicken in the mountains, so I dined on mutton which had seen better days, and fell into bed.

Thankfully, in the morning we found not only the best macaroon shop in town, but a café selling delicious samosas and momos, which are like tiny Cornish pasties.

As we tucked in gratefully, on the mountain beyond stood a trio of brightly painted Buddhist shrines, like those recycling bins you get at home: clean souls in the white one, dirty in the red, and the rest in the green for sorting out later.

And beyond that, the 11th-century mountaintop monastery of Stong-dey, which we rode up to in the afternoon just in time to tiptoe into the courtyard and find the monks, in fantastical robes and hats, entertaining an audience of locals with dancing to the accompaniment of drums, cymbals, and horn.

A junior lama wearing a plumed Victorian helmet bearing the words "Horse Artillery" kept order with a sword, and a grizzled ancient dispensed rancid yak butter from a pouch and rosewater from a McDowell's rum bottle, while two small terrors wearing dragon masks raced about demanding small change or else.

From a raised dais, the Rinpoche sucked on a boiled sweet and surveyed the scene with an expression of either infinite boredom or infinite serenity.

Afterwards, he invited us for tea and biscuits in his inner sanctum, but neither that, nor even the dancing, was the highlight of the day.

No, that was Kunza Lomo, the sweet little six-year-old girl who grasped my hand and wouldn't let go, even when I lifted her high, swung her around until she laughed and cried, and let her try on my bike helmet.

"You know," said Suzie as we hugged her goodbye, "it would only cost £100 a year to pay for her education, and change her life."

"Consider it done," I said.

After all, it's not every day you go for a motorcycle ride and adopt a little girl.

I thought of her much the next day as I rode back along the long and arduous road to Kargil, a Shi'ite Muslim town where a polite request at our hotel as to the possibility of beer somehow led to me jumping into a taxi with Jamal the mechanic, followed by a breakneck ride across town, six whispered phone calls, three false alarms, and finally a secret drinking den down an alleyway filled with guilty-looking sons of Allah.

Two minutes later, an unfeasibly large sum of money had changed hands, and I was scuttling back to the taxi carrying a hessian sack containing a dozen bottles of Godfather Extra Strong.

Our success must have been an omen, for the next day was a glorious run back to Leh in time for curry and cheaper beer, and the day after, the steep and sinuous climb to Khardung Pass, at 18,000 feet loftier than Everest base camp and the highest motorable road in the world.

By now I was constantly amazed at the way the Enfield shrugged off sand, gravel, mud, rocks, ploughed earth at roadworks, and regular torrents of snowmelt which turned the road into a raging river.

Even in the worst of it, you just stood on the pegs, and no matter how much the bike bucked and weaved beneath you, it chugged through everything.

In the afternoon, the track wound down the other side and gradually turned to tarmac. It may have been worse than the worst B road in the UK, but it was heaven to us as it swooped and dived its way down into the Nubra Valley, a symphony of river and sand dunes framed by alpine peaks.

At last we came to the Shangri-La of Hunder, a village of bright temples and beautiful women cradled in an almost Tuscan landscape of mustard fields and poplars.

Greeted by the friendly waves of homecoming workers and schoolchildren, we camped in an apricot wood by a ramshackle monastery occupied by a sole wizened ancient the spitting image of Yoda; although when I say "camped," we were actually in lofty tents with carpeted floors, not to mention hot showers, delicious food, and cold beer around a crackling bonfire.

However, just when we thought the road had thrown everything it had at us, next day the 16,000-foot Wari Pass between Nubra and Pangong Tso was snowbound. In July.

Having slithered and pushed our way through that, we found the road blocked by a broken-down truck. The bikes could get past, but not the backup vehicle.

An hour of exhausting shovelling and rock shifting later, we were through, but it was now teatime, there were another six hours to Pangong Tso, and only the suicidal travel on Indian roads after dark.

"You know, this trip has had so many highlights: Lamayuru, the long road to Rangdum and Padum, the mountains, the glaciers, the scenery, and meeting the Rinpoche, but getting through that snow was both the biggest challenge and the biggest sense of achievement," said an exhausted Peter.

"But it's really inspired me. I'll be back, believe me."

A decision was made: we would stay at Tiksey, just 18 miles away, and the home of a beautifully-restored monastery which I strolled around that evening: a place where you may find peace, if you have it within you.

It was also the perfect base for finally striking out the next day for the last and most exotic destination of the trip: the fabled lake of Pangong Tso, straddling the border between Ladakh and Tibet.

As we rode slowly up the mountain roads in the morning sun, the colours which had become so familiar spread out before us: above us, the aching blue of sky, then the snowy peaks, the mottled brown slopes, the green and yellow of the valley below, and the icy blue of the rushing river which nourished it.

And then, at last, the lake at the end of our long and winding road.

Blessed by sky and cradled by mountains, I looked down at the myriad shades of blue and green in its depths, and in that moment it encapsulated India to me: an exquisite gem as the reward for a thousand miles of heat and dust.

Geoff Hill is a critically acclaimed bestselling author and award-winning feature and travel writer based in Belfast.

As a motorbike columnist for a series of national UK and Irish newspapers, he recently found himself one of the most widely read bike columnists in the UK and Ireland; which is surprising considering that his columns are a desperate attempt to disguise the fact that he knows bugger all about motorbikes.

He's also the editor of Microlight Flying *magazine, in spite of the fact that he knows even less about aeroplanes than he does about motorbikes.*

*He's the author of 10 books, including accounts of epic motorbike journeys from Delhi to Belfast and Route 66 (*Way to Go*), Chile to Alaska (*The Road to Gobblers Knob*), around Australia (*Oz*) and most recently,* In Clancy's Boots, *recreating the journey of Carl Stearns Clancy, the first person to take a motorbike around the world 100 years ago—complete with Clancy's original boots.*

Web: Geoff-Hill-Adventures.com

Twitter: @ghillster

Five Bikes

Mark Richardson

This story has appeared in the Wheels *section of the* Toronto Star.

It almost goes without saying, of course, that every man, woman, and child in this country should own at least five motorcycles: a sport bike, a cruiser, a tourer, a dirt bike, and "something interesting."

Unfortunately, not everyone has the means to make this possible. Garages get cramped, and closets fill rapidly with the different styles of clothing and armour that are needed to dress the part. As well, it can get quite costly, especially since each motorcycle, for some reason, must be individually insured for collision.

Consequently, not everybody actually does own five motorcycles. I myself, for reasons of limited space and funds, own only three and a half. But because one and a half of them are in pieces under my workbench and up in the garage rafters, and the second is now ancient and officially retired from strenuous activity, I have to make do with just the one.

This can be terribly difficult at times. My main motorcycle is a cruiser, a Harley Low Rider, since I'm now of a certain age and have slowed down to smell the roses and drink the (decaffeinated) coffee. There are times, however, when I think about her being something else.

On the way here, for example, a 200-km ride northwest from Toronto, it would have been nice to have ridden in an entourage of motorcycles, swapping back and forth as different opportunities for riding came available.

I know this route well, having taken variations of it over the years to reach Collingwood or Owen Sound, or when heading up to Tobermory to catch the Manitoulin ferry, and no bike can do it all to full potential.

The most exciting ride was probably with the Ontario Dualsport Club a few years ago, heading north on trails and gravel roads to the Ride for Sight campground when the charity event was held outside Collingwood. That was fun. Muddy, too. Not every machine could make it through the bogs and swamps when the official trail kept disappearing under water.

I was riding a Suzuki DR650, monikered the SEX, that year, which broke the ice right away with my newfound dirt-riding friends. We reached the campground tired and filthy, then pitched tents and began drinking. The next morning, still covered in the previous day's mud and feeling tender from the previous night's mood, we rode south and I crashed spectacularly while descending the trail beside the Mansfield ski hill. Ah—good times.

Riding here now on the cruiser, warm sun on my face and strong wind at my flank, I passed a few gravel side roads that promised a lack of maintenance just over the ridge. "Use at your own risk," said the signs. The cruiser kept straight on along the asphalt. Another day, perhaps.

The next year of the Ride for Sight parade up to Collingwood, I rode an extremely fast sport bike, a Honda 929 Fireblade. I lined up at the start meeting point and found myself behind two Harley-Davidsons. When they started their V-twin engines, the pavement rippled from the decibels and the few shreds of baffle mesh left in their mufflers were blown out the tailpipes onto the lot.

I moved discreetly to another line to park behind two Hondas, big Gold Wings, known for their sedan-like quiet and limo-like ride. I don't know if their huge water-cooled engines were running or not. But I do know that as soon as the parade began and the sound of the other motorcycles increased, their radios boosted volume automatically to compensate for the ambient noise.

The whole way north up Airport Road, I sat hunched at the speed limit on the race-ready sport bike, listening to the easy-listening song stylings of Whitney Houston and Billy Joel pumping back at me. And somewhere around Stayner, the heavens opened and I arrived soaked and cold at the campground.

On the way home that year, I opened up the Fireblade and took advantage of the curves south of Creemore and the interesting roads around Cataract, Belfountain, and Georgetown. But there are long, straight stretches that link these sections, and the bike was uncomfortable at anything even approaching legal speeds. I longed for the more upright position of a tourer or even a cruiser over such distance—and I was younger then.

Riding today on the road to Damascus (Ontario) past the Luther Marsh, the wind grows stronger from the west and the horizon there darkens. I've rarely chosen this road, though I used to live nearby in Mount Forest.

Local lore has it that the two townships I'm passing through, Luther and Melancthon, were deemed by their surveyor to be the most ghastly tracts of swampland he'd experienced. A devout Roman Catholic, he named them after the German Protestant reformists Martin Luther and Philipp Melanchthon, whom he considered the most ghastly people imaginable.

On a warm and sunny day, this rarely travelled road is quiet and idyllic. On every other day, with the wind whipping across the fields, it's obvious why the road is little used. It's fine for a cruiser if you're stretched out and relaxed behind a comfortable windshield, but exhausting if there's no fairing and you're fighting the wind with your forearms and the small of your back, as I did a quarter-century ago on my "interesting" Honda CB350F.

Ah, that little 350. What a plucky bike, and I loved her for a while. Not for long, though. I left her to die in a farmer's field when she no longer had any value even to me. No starter, worn-out tires, and a head gasket that just wouldn't seal. Not enough power to fight a strong headwind, unlike the 70 hp or so of my cruiser today, which snicks confidently into sixth gear and lopes comfortably toward the horizon, firing its pistons at every other telephone post.

The road turns west into the wind and through Mount Forest. This town hasn't changed in the many years since I lived here, when I was a recent immigrant and desperately homesick for the winding country lanes I'd left behind in Europe. Midwestern Ontario in the wintertime is not a welcoming place for a young transplanted motorcyclist with aspirations for cafe racing.

I weathered the years with the little Honda, and then with a Kawasaki GPZ750 that I bought for myself on turning 21. Now that was more like it! The police didn't think so, though, and it became clear that the sport bike would have to go.

Just outside the tiny pioneer community of Drew, east of Clifford, it's finally time to check the map. The roads haven't changed, but my memory has. I'm looking for the highway that leads north to Hanover and then up to here, a tiny intersection just outside Chesley. According to ridegreybruce.com, the Harley Blues Cafe in Scone is "a great watering hole," which is as good a reason as any to ride up here on a rare day with an empty schedule. Every journey must have a destination, no matter how vague.

While I'm standing beside the bike at the side of the road, mulling over the map and sheltered from the growing side wind by a copse of trees, a Buick slows and pulls over alongside. Its window winds down. "Are you okay?" asks the woman in the passenger seat. "Do you need any help?" They're good people up here.

Reassured of the route, I ride for a while behind a Gold Wing, its rider in shirtsleeves. A BMW Adventurer passes in the oncoming lane, its rider in Kevlar, and we all wave at each other. The Wing stays west and I turn north through Neustadt, where the wind is now stronger, building with every concession. A Harley passes in the opposite direction, its riders wearing rain gear. The western sky is black.

Scone is still 30 kilometres to the north, but the weather is rushing through. I'm not going to make it.

I've been caught in the rain many times and it's never pleasant, but it's not that big a deal. This is different, though. The wind is picking up dust on Hanover's main street and it's swirling everywhere. People are running for cover. This feels like a tornado's on the way.

There's a Tim Hortons—shelter. I park the bike with its side stand propped against the wind and hurry in; moments after I get inside, the storm hits. Sheets of water sweep the lot. There are no cars moving on the road. This is a big one.

A couple of other motorcyclists scurry inside, caught short on a ride down from Barrie. Their rat bikes are in the lot and a Mazda parks alongside. Two women jump out and hurry to the coffee shop, carrying a baby. They're the riders' partners, following close behind as they all try to escape their cares for the day. To each their own.

Why am I here again, killing time over coffee while the temperature drops outside and the rain washes over everything? To go for a ride, get out of Toronto for a while, relax on the road less travelled as I finally find some time to think over the last 30 years of riding.

Outside the window, the water cascades over my bike's muffler, splashes through the fins on the engine, slips around the paint of the gas tank. I didn't bring any rain gear. The forecast didn't call for rain.

If I had five bikes in the garage, should I have chosen another motorcycle?

Not a sport bike. This ride was supposed to be a loop over to Thornbury where a corner-carver would have excelled, but not today. I'll head back on a shorter loop today.

Not a dirt bike. This is too wet and wild to venture onto the trails. They'll be saturated and—if they're passable—not much fun.

Not an "interesting bike." Riding home in the cold damp will turn into endurance, and that's no element for a vintage machine, or a custom chopper, or a one-off close to the heart.

Maybe a tourer, though. Get me back swiftly and efficiently, dry behind the fairing and warm from the protected riding position. Yes, maybe a tourer.

And the rain's stopped, blown out as rapidly as it blew in. I leave the Tim's to escape its air-conditioned chill. The sky's still overcast. The worst is over, but the cold and the damp aren't going away.

As I ride the last few minutes north, the air is cool against my face and the road is patchy with puddles. But I can stretch out in the comfortable seat—legs forward on the highway pegs, arms resting on the handlebars—and the bike lopes along again. She's dirty now, her chrome dull and her paint grimy, but no different under the surface.

And finally, here at Scone, the Harley Blues Cafe is closed and there's just a sign that says "Open soon." Not to worry—I'm coffee'd out from the Tim's, anyway. And there's no disappointment. Like the T-shirt says, for any decent road trip it's the journey itself that's the destination, not the other way around.

There's no disappointment with the bike, either. Riding a motorcycle is all about finding the right attitude—inside the head, there's plenty of room for five bikes. My cruiser is just about as good a tourer as I want it to be, and more protective against the wind and rain once the windshield is adjusted a little higher. She tips bravely into corners and has no fear riding slowly on gravel roads. And she's my bike, which makes her unique.

It'll take me a couple of hours to get home from here, but that's okay. Outside the closed cafe, I dig out a sweater from the saddlebag and reach for the map. Might as well figure out an interesting route back.

Mark Richardson is the author of Zen and Now, *and* Canada's Road.

Web: ZenAndNow.org
Twitter: @WheelsMark

Return to the Bay of Pigs

Christopher P. Baker

The following in an excerpt from the book Mi Moto Fidel, *published by National Geographic Adventure Press. Used with permission.*

The Autopista Nacional, Cuba's only freeway, is a concrete eight-laner—colloquially called the Ocho Vías—that runs through open countryside east of Havana for 250 miles. Flat as a carpenter's level, it has only a few potholes and the occasional mule-drawn cart or stray cow in the road to contend with. I had the highway virtually to myself as I ran east at 75 miles per hour past green swathes of sugarcane.

Cruising down an empty highway with the rush of warm air caressing my skin stirred sensations of self-reliance and freedom. It was exhilarating to be riding alone, a million light-years from anything familiar. Just me and *mi moto fidel*. I couldn't remember when I had last been so happy.

I was travelling with my duffel farther forward for back support. My shoulders no longer ached. I felt perfectly poised, my ass snug and secure in the saddle as if human and bike had become as one. I was in a kind of highway heaven where heightened awareness merged with the exhilaration of absolute freedom.

I'm a cautious rider, not fast, but that morning I felt the urge to twist the throttle, to thrill to the bike's awesome power and hear the steady beat of the big twin in its glory. I cranked the bike open until the handlebars were quivering.

Then—BLAM! I hit a railway track running across the freeway, hidden deep in the shadow of an overpass. The bike shuddered and I flew through the air like Evel Knievel, smashing down 20 feet farther along the highway. The springs bottomed out; my helmet crashed down on the windshield. I had come down perfectly square, however, and roared forward with my heart racing.

The simultaneous fright and relief made me laugh out loud. Bloody hell! The Paris-Dakar had taken the impact in stride, but I slowed to fifty to regain my composure.

Ahead the gelid sky was turning to pewter, and a storm was gathering in great roiling clouds. There was steel in the wind now buffeting me from the north. Soon the first raindrops began to splatter the windshield. The road gave off moist odours. I stopped and pulled out my rain gear. There was no sign of shelter for miles, so I continued with my head and body bowed low to avoid the pellets that stung my face. Then it really began hammering down. I carried on at a crawl, the rain invading the cuffs of my jacket and creeping up my arms in cold rivulets. Water trickled down my waterproof boots. At least they were warmed by the heat from the cylinders.

An open-bed truck passed. It was laden with passengers huddled shoulder to shoulder against the driving rain like penned-in cattle, so crowded together and wearing such looks of misery that I could not imagine a more disconsolate-looking bunch. Cuba was forever putting my sense of hardship in perspective.

Near Jagüey Grande, the rain let up as quickly as it had begun. Sunlight poured down through gaps in the clouds and steam rose off the highway. I turned into town to dry off and tank up on gas. I passed a *parque de diversiones* where children whirled giddily on mechanical rides. Their gleeful faces lifted my spirits.

Jagüey is an agricultural town, railhead, and crossroads whose junction is a major *botella* (literally "bottle"), the colloquial Cuban term for a post where Cubans gather in droves to hitch rides. Virtually the entire Cuban population relies on the bus system for travel between cities, but demand so exceeds supply—Cuba's bus stations have been called "citadels of desperation"—that there is often a waiting list in excess of one month for the most popular long-distance routes. The gasoline shortage had so worsened things that hitchhiking had become a way of life, and the government had formed a state agency, Inspección Estatal, with officials strategically placed at *botellas* to flag down passing vehicles and fill empty seats democratically. Recognizable by their mustard-coloured uniforms, the officials were called *coges amarillos*—yellow jackets.

Hitchhikers waved beseechingly as I pulled up to inspect a tourist attraction called Finca Fiesta Campesina, with a zoo, a traditional *trapiche* (sugarcane press) and a souvenir shop selling deliciously dulcet Cuban coffee, thick and rich as molasses. A dirt road led into a field behind the finca, where a little village of rustic log-and-thatch cottages had been opened as a homespun "hotel" called Bohío Don Pedro, named for the patriarch around whose farmstead the affair had been built. I parked the bike in gear, on the kickstand, and walked up to the farmhouse. I liked it immediately and decided to stay. The manager, Danilo Canizo, welcomed me warmly, then led me to one of the cozy huts. Randy roosters were chasing chickens around the grounds.

"The parking lot is secure," suggested Danilo in fluent English, "but if you want you can pull your moto onto your veranda."

I did so, but not from paranoia. I wanted my bike where I could see it. I was beat, worn down by the rain and the wind, so I spent the afternoon sprawled in a hammock and stared at my BMW enamelled in the late afternoon sunlight, contemplating it as if it were my lover. I even dropped to the floor and moved around it to admire its muscular curves from a different angle.

A sweet perfume drifted on the warm air, and the only sounds were the thrumming of the bees, the steady cadence of the cicadas, and the rustling of palm fronds from the breeze. A chestnut gelding grazed near-by, adding to the bucolic enchantment. Pigs were grunting and scrapping over slop that Don Pedro was pouring from a rusty bucket. The old farm-er was bare-chested and bronzed, dressed in straw hat and torn trousers, and he chomped on an unlit cigar.

I pulled on a pair of jeans and a denim shirt and joined Danilo. We rocked on the porch outside the kitchen, where Don Pedro's wife, Hildeli-za, was preparing a dinner that smelled strongly of garlic. Together we watched the farm animals feasting while the setting sun gilded the leaves of the alum and mango trees like shimmering foil. With dusk, the cocker-els scattered the leaves as they chased the recalcitrant females.

The scene reminded me of a famous anecdote, apparently true, re-garding ex-president Calvin Coolidge and his wife—who it is said, shared a lacklustre love life. Danilo asked to hear it.

"Well, it appears that the president and his wife visited a farm and were given separate tours. Mrs. Coolidge asked the guide if the rooster copulated more than once a day. 'Dozens of times,' she was told. 'Tell that to the president,' she replied. When Coolidge was told, he inquired if it was with the same hen every time. 'Oh, no, a different one every time,' came the answer. 'Tell that to Mrs. Coolidge,' he replied."

Danilo laughed heartily. I heard Hildeliza chuckling in the kitchen.

"It's beautiful when the chickens and little birds are here at this hour," said Hildeliza, peering out from her workplace. Gaily-coloured songbirds had gathered to drink from the dripping faucet.

I asked Danilo where most of the guests came from.

"The majority are Canadian, but we get plenty of anglers from the United States who come to fish in Laguna Salinas."

"They molest the chickens," Hildeliza added. I thought she was still speaking of the cockerels, but she meant the *yanqui* fishermen, who can't stand the crowing in the morning and throw stones at the *gallos* to chase them away.

Laguna Salinas is part of the vast Zapata swamp, which extends south from Jagüey Grande and smothers the shoe-shaped Zapata peninsula, forming a 4,230-square-kilometre morass—the largest wetland ecosystem in the Caribbean—that is Cuba's foremost wildlife reserve. Zapata envelops the deep, finger-like *Bahía de Cochinos* (Bay of Pigs). The area is considered a sensitive region for more than ecological reasons, and the Cuban government has traditionally kept a tight rein on foreign visitation. But things were easing up, said Danilo, and fishermen were now making a beeline.

"The fish are so numerous here, the waters boil like a kettle," Danilo claimed matter-of-factly. "There are places where you can catch them with your bare hands, the way the Indians did. I've seen it myself. Bonefish here will swim between your legs and not scatter." He disappeared and returned with a brochure for a U.S. company that brings fishermen on prepaid, all-inclusive tours.

We dined in a *bohío* lit by the warm glow of kerosene lamps. Bats wheeled in and out, swerving like intergalactic warships from a battle scene in Star Wars.

I complimented Hildeliza on her cooking.

"But I make the bread!" chimed in Don Pedro.

"It's the best bread in Cuba," his wife added proudly. She asked how I liked Cuba. Her smile broadened when I told her "very much."

An Israeli drip-irrigation expert called Shlomo sat on my right. He was working on an 115,000-acre citrus project nearby. The enterprise was being run by an Israeli company that hoped to increase the quality of the notoriously poor Cuban citrus (most of which previously supplied the Soviet bloc or found its way into juices) to compete on world markets.

"How long before Cuba begins producing fruit as good as Florida's?" I asked.

"They already are," Shlomo replied. "The quantity is small as yet, but they're now producing grapefruits equal in quality to those of Israel. Only about one percent of their total production is export quality. The Cubans claim that it's far higher, but you can't trust any of the official figures. The decimal points get 'accidentally' moved in their annual reports so that managers can show that they've met their production quotas. Once the mistake is made, it becomes fixed. I've challenged the figures several times, but the answer is always the same. 'It must be correct. See, it says twelve percent here!'

"I once saw a report showing *X* number of boxes with 500 kilos of fruit. I knew it was wrong. A box holds 400 kilos. It was impossible to get that much fruit in a box. Know what they said? Cuban citrus are heavier!" He laughed. "They claim that they make a profit. No one knows whether they make a profit or not. Indirect costs aren't taken into account."

I related a joke told by Andres Oppenheimer in his book *Castro's Final Hour* explaining why it was impossible to find pork, the traditional Cuban staple, on supermarket shelves.

"Fidel visits a pig farm and stops to admire a pregnant pig. 'Beautiful specimen,' says Fidel. 'I bet it will produce at least ten piglets.' Everyone applauds and nods in agreement. Fidel leaves. Two weeks later, the pig gives birth but delivers only six piglets. The farm's administrative office is beside itself with panic. The farm manager fears Fidel will be furious at the lower-than-expected production, so he records in his report that the pig delivered seven piglets. His supervisor, the regional farm director, raises the number to eight and passes his report to the national farm director, who changes the figure to nine. His boss, the Minister of Agriculture, adds one more piglet and submits the report personally to Castro. 'Fabulous! Ten piglets!' says Fidel, delighted that his prediction has come true. 'We'll use 60 percent of the pigs for export, and 40 percent for domestic consumption.'"

The trio had already heard it. They laughed anyway.

Two other guests—husband and wife Spanish tourists—were watching a video replay of their visit to the Bay of Pigs. They passed the camera around the table.

On the tape, crabs the size of dinner plates crawled up the banks and went click-clacking across the road. The wife pinned one with a big stick, picked it up from behind, and held it up to the camera. Fearsome claws waved directly in my face.

"Every mid-March the crabs begin gathering in the mangroves for vast orgies and egg-laying parties," said Danilo. "First come the really big ones on their way to lay eggs in the sea. At the end, the newborn crabs make their way ashore. Hence, we says it's a smaller problem in April. There are probably 100,000 *cangrejos* crossing the road as we speak. You're going to have problems with the moto," he added ominously. "It's crazy to go in a motorcar. Think what it's like on a motorcycle. I can put all the money in the world on the table you'll not make it."

"True? Or are you kidding?"

"True!"

I studied the video again. The road was littered with broken shells and upturned pincers. My mind turned to punctures. I thought for a moment about skipping the Bay of Pigs and continuing east along the *Autopista*, but that seemed like touring Paris without visiting the Eiffel Tower.

"If you hit a log, just keep going," said Don Pedro, smirking gleefully. "It could be a crocodile!" He gripped my hand and hugged me before wishing me "*¡Buenos sueños!*" Sweet dreams!

I lay awake for a while, listening to the gallimaufry of tooting whistles and clanking engines and carriages drifting across the cane fields from the local central, where sugarcane was being unloaded around the clock.

* * *

The road ran south like a plumb line past endless miles of dark-green sawgrass and reeds swaying in the wind. I arrived at Playa Larga, a small fishing village tucked into the head of the 20-kilometre-long bay where 1,297 heavily armed CIA-trained Cuban exiles had come ashore in April

1961 to establish a beachhead and incite a counterrevolution that would topple the Castro regime (Cubans refer to the battle site as "Playa Girón"). Concrete monuments lined the roadside. Each one marked the site where a member of the Cuban military—161 in all—had fallen defending *la revolución* during the three-day battle. I passed a youth camp and through the corner of my eye caught the unflinching gaze of a young communist pioneer peering down from his watchtower.

Farther south came the crabs. The gravel road was strewn with crustaceans squashed flat by vehicles, like giant M&Ms crushed underfoot. Their black carapaces littered the path ahead and my route was patterned in pointillist dots. I dodged around them, avoiding the margins where the razor-sharp shards and pincers of partially-crushed crabs stuck up like broken bottles. The air stank of fetid crabmeat. Vultures hopped about, drawn greedily to the prodigal banquet.

I passed my first live crab—bright orange—scurrying toward the sea. Then a large black crab with terrifying red pincers ran across my path, the forerunner of a lethal invasion heading the other way. Suddenly I was surrounded by a battalion of armoured, surly crustaceans that turned to snap at my tires. I slalomed between them as they rose in the road with menacing claws held high. Then I hit one square on. POOF! It sounded like bubble wrap exploding.

Finally I arrived at the climactic spot where socialism and capitalism had squared off. Cuban families and Canadian package tourists slathered with suntan oil splashed about in the turquoise shallows. My black leathers and boots must have looked absurd. I gave one of the Cubans my camera and asked him to snap a shot of me leaning against the bike in front of a huge billboard reading "PLAYA GIRÓN—THE FIRST ROUT

OF IMPERIALISM IN LATIN AMERICA." It was difficult, with the sun beating down on a beach as white as mountain snow, to imagine that blood and bullets had mingled with the sand and the surf here 35 years before.

Christopher P. Baker, Lowell Thomas Award Travel Journalist of the Year in 2008, is a professional travel writer/photographer and moto-journalist whose literary travelogue Mi Moto Fidel: Motorcycling Through Castro's Cuba *is a two-time national book award winner. He is acknowledged as the world's foremost authority on Cuba travel and culture, about which he has written and photographed six books, including* Cuba Classics: A Celebration of Vintage American Automobiles. *His feature articles on motorcycling have appeared in publications as diverse as* Adventure Motorcyclist, BMW Motorcycle, CNN Travel, Motorcyclist, National Geographic Traveler *and* Robb Report. *He appears frequently on radio and television talk shows and has appeared on ABC, BBC, CNN, Fox TV, the National Geographic Channel, NBC, and NPR. Christopher is a contributing photographer to, and Resident Expert for,* National Geographic. *He leads group motorcycle tours of Cuba for MotoDiscovery (MotoDiscovery.com).*

Web: ChristopherPBaker.com

A Two-Wheeled Vision Quest

Nicole Espinosa

The fog swirled in, swiftly covering any recollection of a beacon. No matter which way I turned my head, I couldn't shake the thick invasion. Direction became murky as I tried to rely on intuition as my inner GPS. I heard the voices of my loved ones calling to me from different locations, but the sounds of home faded into the distance. I was lost … and I hadn't even left my head.

As I slipped further into the automation of daily routine, the idea that it had been three years since my last solo weighed heavily. There was just one prescription to lift that "fog," and that could only be made by the road doctor—Jack B. Nimble, my DRZ.

His prescription: "Three weeks on the road, solo, where I'm the needle, and you are the thread, as we stitch together the most beautiful tapestry of connection with nature, with friends, with ourselves."

"As usual, Jack, you're a wise little bike. Think I'll take heed."

And out the door we flew, after kissing my angels goodbye. You see, my kids have grown up knowing how important these journeys are to me, and to them. They get to witness me living life in a bigger way, and are embracing it for themselves. There will come a day when they, too, will spread their wings and have the confidence to find the highest thermals.

For some reason, I hadn't been drawn to sit down with the maps to flesh out a route. The only things set in stone were the homes of loving friends who were waiting for me to make my way to them in Arizona and Colorado. The pull that I felt strongly, though, was the desire to fly by the seat of my pants and leave it all to serendipity—a decision that would chart a journey of the heart. At every turn, friends, strangers, and circumstance would nudge me in the direction I needed to follow to fill my soul.

My first day on the road felt like I wasn't soloing at all. I was in the company of trusted friends—familiarity, excitement, freedom, and oneness. This was the usual posse who joined me on all my solos, but there is always one specific element that is just as important as armour on these trips—self-sufficiency. In addition to the streamlined kits that allow me to survive on my own, I added an HD video camera, solar charger, and netbook. I took on the challenge of videoing this journey, hoping to capture innermost desires and revelations from myself, others, and the landscape. Oh, yeah, I know it adds at least quadruple the road time to set up the shots, turn on the camera, go back to enter the frame cleanly, stop beyond, come back to retrieve the camera, and so on. And, invariably around the next corner, there's a more beautiful piece of scenery to capture. The blooper reel will be hilarious, as I had to run back to get the camera, huffing and puffing in moto gear and helmet, over and over again. It was all so worth the effort to capture these gems of authenticity.

My first night's destination was a remote campground at the Painted Rock Petroglyph site just northwest of Gila Bend, AZ. Having this place all to myself, I felt a deep sense of ancient history from the Indian tribes and long-ago explorers who left their inscriptions in the rock. After a quick camp set-up, I scrambled up the volcanic rock formations to catch the petroglyphs by twilight. The past surrounded me in a way I had never felt before, giving me the sense that I actually had the power to help create new history for my civilization, by helping to make our tomorrow a better place. Later that night, after slipping into my Big Agnes sleeping bag, I reflected further on how to effect change in this world. As I drifted off to sleep, I realized it would be through finding ways of giving back, and inspiring others to live life more fully. What a powerful way to start this journey.

I knew the next leg would test my dirt riding and navigational abilities. I also knew that staying open to the way the adventure unfolded would keep me flowing with the current rather than rowing against it.

Friends Roseann and Jonathan Hanson, founders of Overland Expo, invited me to stay with them on their 23-acre off-the-grid Arizonan desert oasis. From the screenshot of marked and unmarked roads that they emailed me, I felt confident that I could find them. But after passing the last bit of asphalt, I ended up deep in unmarked dirt-road territory, circling around for two hours in cavernous washouts, ruts, baby-head boulder fields, and 30-foot soft sand pits. I needed an alternative solution. I had a SPOT satellite messenger, but didn't want to press the help button just yet.

I flagged down the first car that happened by within a two-hour period. "I'm trying to find Roseann and Jonathan Hanson on Cloverfield Road. Do you happen to know where that is?"

The husband looked at me quizzically, then responded, "No, I can't say that I do."

His wife smiled and gently backhanded his shoulder as she said, "We live on Cloverfield Road!"

He laughed. "All I know is that I live next to a big cactus." And we all had a chuckle as they pointed in the direction of the Hansons'.

I finally made it to my friends' hideaway. Over the course of one of the most beautiful desert evenings I have ever encountered, these dear souls taught me the nobility of leaving a small footprint on this earth. I fell asleep in the guest tent adorned with African handiwork, while I dreamt of building my own future off-the-grid home.

The next morning as I returned to the pavement I was proud of myself for staying upright through the torturous dirt-riding test with such a big load. Almost back to the tarmac, and on my way to visit Michael Battaglia of the famed Tucson motorcycle shop, On Any Moto, I realized I'd forgotten to put on my deodorant. As I flicked down the side stand, pulled my backpack around and took care of business, a sudden gust of wind pushed the bike past an inch of what my leg could hold and over it went. Would I be able to get myself out of this predicament without anyone else around? I'd have to unload the little beast so I could get it lifted, and I decided to film the process, but then the video camera ran out of battery juice, adding to the comedy of errors. It was quite a feat when all was said and done. I sure hope Michael and crew appreciated how great I smelled by the time we cruised into Tucson.

With a new pair of Dunlop D606 shoes from On Any Moto, I rolled on to the quaintest of hillside towns: Bisbee, AZ. It was another gorgeous day of Arizona riding as I pulled up at sunset to my friend Grant Sergott's custom hat shop, Optimo Hatworks. Grant knows the ultimate scenic back roads of Arizona, New Mexico, Colorado, and Utah like the back of his hand, and he took it upon himself to map out my entire route.

For this, I will be ever grateful. The landscape that these roads took me through was life-changing, and the most powerful experience there landed me in Navajo territory for a couple of days, at the Canyon de Chelly National Monument in northern Arizona.

Here I became fast friends with Howard, the Navajo owner of Spider Rock Campground, and took advantage of the culinary skills of his grandchildren, who were busy cranking out fry bread. That evening, I topped mine off with butter and powdered sugar, the perfect dessert after wolfing down a homemade rehydrated East Indian dinner while watching the Sunset Channel on Mother Nature's big-screen TV. The next morning, I set out early—my backpack stuffed with camera, tripod, camp chair, and lunch—to discover the rim trail, which took me right to the expansive canyon striated with grades of red rock. Having this natural splendour all to myself was beyond anything I could have imagined, and it gave me a deep sense of clarity, with visions of the future as if I were already walking it.

Within this vision, I saw a greater tomorrow that's growing exponentially. So many people are creating ripples of action that turn into huge waves of change. The concept of the "butterfly effect," where the flapping of a butterfly's wings might affect the outcome of weather across the continent, inspired me for the rest of the trip. No matter the size of the action, the people it touches will pay it forward into a larger wave of compassion. The idea played itself out in a small way when I donated my time at the Thodenasshai Navajo Shelter Home. It was at this shelter that I helped Ron Grace's Lost for a Reason charity deliver direly-needed supplies to women and children. As I looked into the eyes of the four-year-old Navajo boy trying on a new jacket that would get him through the winter, I saw the future of humanity dance.

I carried the image of the boy's new outlook with me on the rest of the trip as if it were wrapped in the most precious of satchels. This is how the clarity from Canyon de Chelly would play itself out. I would no longer have to cut my adventures short to rush home to my children, because I couldn't stand experiencing the depth of life without them. Instead, I'd figure out a way to take them with me, so this precious satchel of hope could be delivered by hand all over the world.

The vision of taking my children with me on a round-the-world expedition in a sidecar completely consumed me the last portion of my trip. I launched off at 3 am the final morning so I could zip home in time to smother them with kisses before they took off for school. As I pulled into a driveway that would become a faded memory within a couple of years' time, I leapt off the bike to sweep them up in my arms to feel our love as one. And just beyond this embrace, as I felt its power growing, was a butterfly in the garden gently opening and closing its wings to the sound of our laughter.

Watch for Nicole, Alana, and Dimitri's worldly sidecar adventures at SidecarSafari.com. You can find additional insights from Nicole, AD-VRider ride reports, and how to dehydrate your own food on her blog at RuggedRider.com, on Facebook as Nicole Stavro Espinosa, Rugged Rider, and Sidecar Safari, and on YouTube as Nicole Espinosa and Sidecar Safari.

Robbers! Robbers! Robbers!

Jordan and Sandra Hasselmann

It is interesting to look back at the decisions one makes to see the chain reaction of cause and effect.

We had spent the last two weeks in the lovely Guatemalan city of Xela attending language school, visiting local markets, and enjoying the luxuries of "city living." We were getting spoiled, so it was time to get back with the program and get back on the bikes. It had been more than four months since Sandra and I had left our home in Calgary and set out on our motorcycle trip to the tip of South America. We had enjoyed the break from the daily grind of packing and unpacking, but we both knew it was now time to make a move. Our old 650cc overland bikes were already kind of beat up before we left, with a dented pannier here and a scratch there, but they seemed to be handling the back roads of Mexico and Central America very nicely. They were also great conversation starters. Whenever we stopped in small villages or by the side of the road, we'd always get peppered with questions about what we were doing, where we were from, and where we were going. If you want to be the centre of attention, just ride a big motorbike in Central America: you will become very popular. We had loved riding around the Mexican volcanoes a few weeks earlier in Iztaccíhuatl and Popocatépetl National Park, so we decided to change our original plan of visiting the colonial town of Antigua, and instead set our course for the volcano-ringed Lago de Atitlán (Lake Atitlan) in hopes of riding, hiking, and paddling for a few days.

The ride to Lago de Atitlán was rainy, but short and easy. We had chosen a route that would take us directly to the village of San Pedro on the west side of the lake, but we missed the unmarked turnoff. We had stopped the bikes to consult our map and consider our options when two Triumph Tigers with Guatemalan plates roared past and then pulled off the highway 50 metres ahead of us. We rode up to them and found Roger, a Kiwi travelling on his own from Guatemala to Argentina. He was with the local Triumph sales manager on a short trip together to put a few kilometres on Roger's new travel bike. They confirmed that we had in fact missed the turnoff, but assured us that there was a much better road to the lake just around the corner. However, this road went to Panajachel, a town located on the opposite side of the lake from San Pedro, and since there was no direct road linking Panajachel to San Pedro, we'd have to take the winding scenic route around the entire lake to reach our destination. Since it was getting late and the rain was now pouring down, they suggested we find a hotel in Panajachel for the night and head to San Pedro in the morning. We *decided* to take their advice instead of sticking to our original plan and rode off into the storm.

As we followed the switchbacks down into Panajachel, it started to clear up and we enjoyed the twisty road which led to one of the most beautiful views in the Americas. From a thousand metres above Lago de Atitlán we were able to take in the whole spectacle: lush volcanic forests; a series of small villages lining the shore; the blue, blue water of the lake; and, of course, the sleeping volcanos for which the region is famous. We found Panajachel to be a bit too big and loud for our tastes: there were a lot of tourist shops and too many other gringos there, many of whom appeared to be looking for adventure after one too many *cervezas*. We couldn't argue about the location, though. Lago de Atitlán is gorgeous! Since we were only there for the night, we tried to make the best of it. We had a shower, dug out some dry clothes, and walked out into the night. We surprised ourselves by having an excellent evening out; we found some great Italian food in a romantic restaurant with live music.

The road around Lago de Atitlán is well known to travellers for a number of reasons: the lake is beautiful, it is ringed with cute towns with amazing vistas, and there are at least four massive volcanoes in the immediate area. Plus we had heard it was a great motorcycling road, so it met our trip-planning criteria. We had also heard that it could be dangerous. Our research had turned up numerous stories of landslides and robberies, but nothing in the past year or so. With this in mind, we stopped by the police station on our way back to the hotel to ask about the road conditions and the security situation. After we reviewed the map with the police officer on duty and described our intended route, he told us it would be perfectly safe, as long as we travelled by day. We briefly talked about retracing our steps and following our original plan of using the direct route to San Pedro from the main highway, but we were looking forward to the twisty roads around Lago de Atitlán, and now that we knew it was safe, we *decided* to take the scenic route around the lake.

We woke up early to get a head start on the day, and as we packed up our motorbikes near the beach, and old fisherman stopped by to chat. He told us he thought the road was too dangerous for us to travel, and that for a small fee, he could transport us and our bikes across the lake to San

Pedro. He used his hand to mime a pistol to make it clear that we was taking about banditos; however, since we'd just been cleared by the police the night before, we thought it was just part of a rather persuasive sales pitch and we *decided* to decline his kind offer.

Once we set out, we were glad we had once again chosen the road less travelled, and the route was everything we hoped it would be. We rode up, down, and around like we were on a roller-coaster through the volcanic region as we circumnavigated the lake en route to San Pedro. On top of all of that, after a week of solid rain, the sun was shining, the rain had stopped, and there was nothing but blue skies. We passed through numerous villages along the way, riding by their small central plazas and well-kept churches and waving to kids running on the sidewalk. Since we'd started early, we even had time to stop for lunch and chat with some of the locals. In short, it was a perfect Sunday ride.

According to our map, the pavement ended right after the town of Santiago Atitlán; however, we knew there was a trail that continued to San Pedro. This five kilometres of "road" had never been paved and had more or less been left to the jungle to maintain. It looked rough … but it looked like fun. Just out of town a big soccer game was in progress, and the players and fans all turned to us and waved, smiled, and gave us the thumbs-up as we rolled by, further validating our decision to take the scenic route. The terrain was steep and bumpy, and the recent rains had left it in a rough and muddy state; soon, we were standing on the pegs pretending to be off-road superstars. There was no traffic, and we stopped often on the track for photos and to take turns riding past each other for the video camera. The bikes struggled for grip in the soft red mud, but we somehow managed to navigate across the ruts and rocks and we started making progress. One thing became clear. It would be a long five kilometres.

The road continued to get worse, but we were riding hard and having a good time, and probably not paying enough attention to our surroundings. Soon enough, the road turned really bad, becoming steeper and much rockier. We considered turning around and heading back the way we had come, but we decided to push on. It might have started out as fun, but now we were quickly running out of riding skill and my tires were essentially bald after more than 22,000 kilometres on the road. I was losing traction on a regular basis and had to push the bike a couple of times. I finally came to a stop trying to get through an especially large rut and Sandra stopped just behind me. I was looking down at the spinning rear wheel, trying to get some traction, and was about to ask Sandra if she would kind enough to dismount and give me a push, when her voice came blaring over the intercom, "Robbers! Robbers! Robbers!"

I looked to my left and sure enough, there they were, two small but stocky men running down the hill with handguns and machetes. Unlike gentlemanly highwaymen of days gone by, these banditos did not yell "Stand and deliver!" nor did they allow me the opportunity to get off my trusty steed. They simply ran up to me and pushed me and my poor bike over. As I was falling, I could see the second robber run over to Sandra's bike. He was waving his machete in one hand and had a handgun in the other, but I could have sworn his gun was made out of wood …. He tucked it into his pants quickly as he grabbed hold of Sandra's bike. It took me a moment to extricate myself from under the motorcycle. I could smell the burning plastic from my riding pants as they melted on the exhaust pipe and I could feel the weight of the machine on my leg.

I lay there for a moment with a very bad feeling in the pit of my stomach. My only thought was "What the hell have we done?" When I finally emerged from under the bike, I was met by a masked man who had not only a machete, but also the business end of a pistol pointed at me. And although I'm no expert, his gun did not look like a piece of wood. In fact, from where I was standing, it looked pretty damn real.

I nervously looked over to Sandra. She was already well into the negotiating process with her robber. Although we had just completed an intensive two-week Spanish language class, we must have missed the module on "Robbery Spanish," because we did not know any of the associated vocabulary. She had somehow managed to convince him that allowing her to park her bike would be better than pushing her over. She then informed him through what seemed like a bizarre combination of baby-Spanish, sign language, and interpretive dance that she would be parking and getting off her bike on her own terms. That seemed to work pretty well. Critically, her actions and calm demeanour set the tone with the robbers for the next five minutes.

Although we were separated, we were still wearing all of our protective gear, which made us feel a little bit safer. I hoped our big jackets, heavy boots, and leather gloves would make us look bigger and less vulnerable. Our helmets had wireless intercoms, and we were able to talk to each other, making sure we were both okay while trying to keep each other calm. Things were happening very quickly, and the intercoms allowed each of us to overhear at least some of what the other was saying to their robber, which was also very useful. We tried to coordinate our actions and stay within sight of each another.

When we travel, we only keep two or three days' worth of cash with us at any given time, and we always carry a "mugger" wallet with fake ID, expired credit cards, and a little cash specifically for this type of situation. Sadly, we had just gone to the bank that morning on the way out of town and I had neglected to move the majority of our money, along with my bank and credit cards, from my mugger wallet to the safety of my real wallet. So when my robber put his gun away to empty my pockets, he found my fake wallet with my real bank and credit cards, my iPod, and the real $80 I had withdrawn earlier that day. He also took my camera with all of our superstar riding videos, so you will have to take my word on our off-road riding prowess.

We could see that our robbers were very nervous; they kept looking over their shoulders and speaking to each other in a very excited manner. It was clear they wanted this transaction to be over as soon as possible. The same could have been said for us.

I decided to follow Sandra's lead and negotiate with my robber. He looked a bit confused at first when I asked for my things back, but he eventually agreed to give me back my bank and credit cards and my iPod if I let him keep the $80 and the camera. All things considered, it seemed like a pretty good deal. After all, he was still brandishing a machete. Since he had already thrown away my fake wallet, I got that back as a bonus.

Over the intercom, I could hear a struggle going on. I turned around to find Sandra holding one end of the duffel bag and her robber pulling on the other. Having gone through the contents of her tank bag, Sandra's robber took the opportunity to demonstrate that although his gun may have been a prop, his machete was very much the real deal. He easily cut though the straps holding her large duffel bag to the back of her bike (the gouges from the machete blade can still be seen on the aluminum luggage rack) and pulled the bag to the ground.

My robber and I watched their duffel bag tug-of-war for a moment; I think both of us were equally impressed, and maybe a little alarmed, at how this little *chica* was handling the robbery. This distraction gave me the opportunity to walk up and take the bag away from both of them, like an angry parent taking away a toy from two fighting children. I carried the bag back to my motorbike, which was still lying on the ground. I noticed that although my bike had stalled during my fall, the ignition and lights were still on. I bent down and honked the horn. This had an immediate effect on the robbers. Over the radio, I told Sandra to do the same, and before long the bandits were backing away from us as if we were the ones with the machetes.

They looked genuinely scared. I don't know what the punishment for robbing tourists at gun/machete-point is in Guatemala, but by the way they looked, I'm willing to bet it's pretty severe. I'm usually not one to court confrontation, but with the stress of the situation, the sound of the horns ringing cross the jungle, and the look of fear in the eyes of our robbers, something came over me and I took a run at the robbers. They took off like they were running for their lives as I chased them back to the jungle. The foliage was so thick that they disappeared into the bushes immediately; however, my bravado ran out at the side of the trail and I did not consider following them any further. The good news was that as they were running, they dropped almost everything they had stolen from Sandra's tank bag, including her prescription eyeglasses, her only warm sweater, and one of their own machetes! The bad news was that they kept the $80 and the camera, and I had potentially risked my life for a pair of glasses, an old sweater, and a beat-up machete ….

We weren't sure what was going on. Our hearts were racing and we were afraid the robbers might come back, possibly with friends, so we wanted to get the hell out of there as fast as possible. I quickly collected the dropped items and Sandra repaired her luggage straps and reloaded her bike. She then helped me right my bike and I lashed the machete to the side. We took off up the hill at what seemed like race pace and promptly crashed. Then we crashed again. And so it went until we reached the top of the hill.

After a couple of hundred metres, we saw a truck parked on the side of the road. It was the police and we finally felt a moment of relief. Even though they had been parked just around the corner, they were not aware of what was going on and had not heard our blaring horns through the dense jungle. Their close proximity certainly helped explain why the robbers were so afraid. When we explained what had happened, they informed us that robberies did happen from time to time on this road which is why the police from Panajachel offer a free escort for tourists over this section of the road.

I couldn't believe what I had just heard! A free police escort through the one dangerous stretch of road in the entire area? Hadn't we just asked the police in Panajachel about the security situation the night before? We had, and they did not mention anything about danger or bandits or a free police escort. Had the police in Panajachel correctly informed us about the possibility of danger on the road, we might have made some different decisions. Had they told us about the free police escort, we would definitely have taken them up on their offer. Sadly, they hadn't done either of those things. We were already angry about being robbed, but when we learned that the police in Panajachel hadn't told us about the escort, we were really upset.

We finally made it to San Pedro and found a gorgeous lakefront hotel that had been recommended by a fellow traveller a few days earlier. Although it was way out of our budget, we checked in and enjoyed a stiff shot of local liquor offered up by the owners; Sandra put ice on her now-swollen ankle that had come from one of her post-robbery crashes, and we waited for the local police so we could give an official statement. They basically repeated everything the police in the jungle had told us: the road has occasional bandits and they offer a free police escort for tourists in the area. They could not understand why the police in in Panajachel hadn't properly informed us and they apologized for the oversight.

Although we were shaken up by the incident, we never really felt personally threatened by the bandits. We could tell they were just poor plantation workers capitalizing on an opportunity, not displaced military or professional thugs. We know others who have travelled that road since without incident, but, as bad as we felt afterward, most of our disappointment and anger was with the police in Panajachel. We felt we had done the right thing and requested advice from the local authorities before making a decision, but I guess sometimes that is not enough.

In the end we *decided* that we liked San Pedro and the area around Lago de Atitlán; in fact, we liked it quite a bit. It was relaxed and cool, and it had a nice vibe. We understood that this type of thing could happen anywhere, even back home in Canada, and it certainly wasn't a reflection of our time in Guatemala. On the contrary, the Guatemalans we met were very welcoming, often inviting us into their homes, pointing out the local sights, or asking about our families. Everyone who helped us after the robbery was very sympathetic and apologized profusely for the incident.

With this in mind, we decided we wouldn't let something thing like a petty holdup change our thoughts on travel, on seeking out the unbeaten path, or on interacting with the locals.

After an evening of relaxing in the lovely lakeside gardens of our hotel, we decided to stay for a few days to recover from our adventure. As it turned out, our Guatemalan adventure was far from over, as this particular decision coincided with the arrival of Tropical Depression E12, a national state of emergency, a flooded harbour, washed-out roads, massive landslides, destroyed bridges, closed highways, large-scale power outages, overflowing rivers, and gale-force winds. Cause and effect? Who knows, but since we were going to be there for a while, we stocked up on wine, beer, and books, got comfortable, and enjoyed the amazing view from hotel. God knows there are worse places to be stuck during a storm.

Jordan and Sandra Hasselmann left their home in Calgary, Alberta in the spring of 2011 for a 14-month motorcycle trip of the Americas, from Calgary to Ushuaia and back (via Newfoundland). They visited 15 countries and travelled more than 47,000 kilometres on their trusty but somewhat beat-up BMW F650Gses. Although Jordan had been riding for seven years prior to the trip, Sandra left with less than 3,500 km of experience, learning how to a ride a motorcycle specifically for the trip to Tierra del Fuego. In addition to riding motorbikes, Jordan and Sandra are enthusiastic travellers, hikers, skiers, snowshoers, and backpackers. They try to spend as much time in the backcountry as possible. Both Jordan and Sandra were born and raised in the heart of the continent, in Winnipeg, Manitoba, Canada, and have lived in Alberta since 2004.

Nowhere to Go

Jeremy Kroeker

The following is an adaptation from the book Through Dust and Darkness, *published by Rocky Mountain Books (RMBooks.com).*

Ar-Raqqa is a city rooted along the banks of the Euphrates River in Syria that smells of dust and cigarette smoke, especially at night. Picking my way along the sidewalk, I stepped over lifts in broken pavement, then back onto the dirty road as a shopkeeper squeegeed out the brown waste-water from his floor.

I never intended to visit Ar-Raqqa. In fact, I never meant to visit Syria in the first place. I wanted to ride my motorcycle, a sun-bleached Kawa-saki KLR 650, from Germany into Iran. But when visa problems prevent-ed me from reaching Iran before heavy snows choked off the mountain pass from Turkey, I headed south. So I carried on now, without direction. Without purpose. I guess that's the only way someone ends up in Ar-Raqqa.

I entered a teahouse. Fluorescent lights flickered overhead, and framed posters of President Bashar al-Assad hung on the green walls. After finding a table, I sat down on a plastic chair to order a narghile. I drew a long breath through the mouthpiece on the water pipe, filling my lungs with cool, white smoke and exhaling the taste of apples. At least I've finally arrived in the Middle East, I thought. Although I had entered the region when I crossed the black water of the Bosporus River in Istanbul, the complex aromas of Europe carried on the wind for hundreds of miles. Out here, though, in Ar-Raqqa, it was simple—sweet smoke and sweet tea. And then there was the dust. You could always smell the dust.

In the morning, a dull orange glow had settled on the city. Rolling my motorcycle out of the hotel lobby and into the street, I clipped my plastic luggage in place before taking a good look around. Concrete buildings blocked my view of the horizon, but overhead I could see a patch of blue, like faded denim on an otherwise burlap sky.

I glanced down at the map folded into the clear plastic pocket of my tank bag. There, the Euphrates River showed up as a clean blue line, but as I rode back over the water toward the highway, it appeared ugly and grey. Everything looked grey, in fact, as a hectoring wind lifted dust from the desert into the atmosphere where it blocked out the sun. Maybe I should have turned back at that point, but here in the valley alongside the river things didn't seem so bad. After considering my options for a moment, I clicked on my left signal light and turned onto the highway, riding east.

From a nearby minaret I could hear the faint wail of the day's second call to prayer. Combined with the crackle of sand against my helmet from the storm, it sounded like a weak signal on an AM radio. The prayer soon faded as I rode out of range, but a circle of blue sky remained above me like a halo. I took that to be a good omen. I carried on through a hot wind that swept up from the south until I came to another town.

Rebar stuck up from flat roofs on cinderblock buildings here. Men squatted together on the ground, sipping tea from clear glasses and sheltering in the entrance of a darkened machine shop. Every street that intersected the highway was either made of dirt, or covered in dirt. One could hardly say. A row of concrete power poles ran along the main road. Their hooded streetlights refused to blink on in spite of the growing darkness.

I pulled over in the lee of a building for a rationed swallow of water. With the fingers of my leather glove I brushed away the film of dust from the map pocket to see where I was, but I couldn't find this town. Not that it mattered, I suppose. I had no destination. What was the point of finding my place on the map if I didn't know where I was going? When I turned away from Iran, I got lost. Now, it occurred to me, I was lost all the time.

I eyed the road; the concrete power poles that followed it vanished behind a curtain of earth. As I strapped up my helmet, an unexpected shiver ran through my body. I glanced around to see if I could find a hotel, but this town was too small. There was that machine shop where the men crouched in the doorway. There was a rusty tractor parked in front of some buildings with overhead metal doors, all rolled down and locked. I couldn't stay here. Besides, it didn't feel right to quit riding for the day. There's the problem with having no destination. It's hard to stop.

Riding out of town, I crested a gentle slope and left the protection of the river valley. Suddenly the storm, having given fair warning, descended upon me with all its wrath. Dust billowed in through the helmet vents, swirling about inside the visor. The edge of my nostrils caked with dirt, bringing with it that horrible dry odour that forces men of the prairies to pray. I resisted the urge to moisten my lips, but when I could bear it no more I took in a mouthful of grit that crunched against my teeth. Every movement of my body, every turn of the head, every articulation of a joint felt like scraping nails on a chalkboard. Tears rolled down my cheeks, collecting sand to deposit in the tangles of my beard. Lifting my eyes, I hoped to find comfort in my blue halo of sky, but it was gone—buried beneath a layer of sediment.

Out here I could only see two dotted lines on the road beyond the front wheel. The needle on my speedometer touched 25 miles per hour, but even that was too fast. For there, emerging before me as a villain through the fog of a nightmare, stood a monstrous tree. Brakes screaming, sand between pad and rotor, I skidded to a stop. I would have hit the tree still—if it hadn't been moving along in my direction.

Thank God for that. Where the thick trunk met the ground, where the roots ought to be, this tree had wheels. Now, as I idled behind it, I could see that this tree was really just a large vehicle spilling over with brushwood.

Peering around it with my head over the dotted line, I saw two trailers hitched to a big-wheeled tractor. As I sighted along the trailers, even the machine pulling them blurred into the storm. Aware that Syrian drivers never use their headlights, I understood the blind risk of an attempt to pass.

My headlight would never penetrate this cloud, but I switched it to high anyway before rolling on the throttle. Looking up as I passed, I saw the driver squinting into the wind, his dark robes flapping, his kafiya wrapped tightly around his head. I pulled back in front of the tractor just as an oncoming transport truck swept along, its dark mass creating turbulent eddies of sand that shook the bike. The driver flashed his lights at me, not as a warning, but to remind me that my headlight was on and that I should switch it off.

Slowing the pace after that, I kept to the centre line to avoid drifts of sand creeping in from the right. I shouldered the bike into the wind, leaning hard to resist the fate of every plastic bag that whipped across our path. Some bags snagged on low thorny bushes, where they billowed out and shredded in the wind. Others must have been carried off into Turkey. With such a dramatic lean, though, the front wheel had a tendency to skip sideways, just an inch or so. Every time it happened my whole body went rigid. I slowed some more.

I reached down to pat the silver gas tank on the old bike, now marked with red pits and scratches from the sand. This storm would be hard on the machine in other ways, too. I thought about the foam air filter. By now it must be as black as a cancerous lung on a cigarette pack. I would have to soak it in gasoline tomorrow, squeezing out the dirt until it returned to the colour of butterscotch pudding. I would let it dry and then coat it with fresh oil. And the chain. That must be a mess. I would scrub every link with diesel fuel. I would adjust the tension and carefully lubricate it. I would do all of these things, I thought, and take better care of the bike in the future. First we needed to get out of this wind.

After four hours, I had only covered ninety miles to reach a major centre. I pulled in at a lonely fuel station outside of city limits. After fuelling up, I parked the bike and slid out of the saddle. Stumbling forward and with shaking hand, I reached for a screen door that opened into a brick cafeteria swarming with sickly houseflies. With the brush of my arm, half a dozen of them fell from the seat, dead or unconscious. A few survivors dropped to the floor and walked away.

The snack bar had little to offer. More to the point, it had no water. I bought a blood-warm bottle of Syrian pop that only mocked my thirst.

I choked down a bag of potato chips and another of dry cookies that turned to a chalky paste inside my mouth. When perhaps the last fly that could still take to the air landed on the lip of my bottle, I tried to shoo it away. Instead it dropped into the drink, dead.

I didn't feel so good myself. I sat at the table for a long time, watching the lazy flies, listening to the screen door as it banged against the frame. Dark-haired men with thick moustaches sat around another table, smoking cigarettes. People went in and out of a small prayer room off to the side, removing their shoes at the door.

I wondered what I should do. I could find a hotel if I rode into the city, but I had it in mind to reach Palmyra for night. Earlier I had spotted it on the map when I stopped to drain the last swallow of water from my bottle. This was a tourist map, the kind with pictures on it to show you where to go. On paper, Palmyra appeared as a green hollow in the desert with a pool of water surrounded by date palms. Yes, I could find shelter in the city, but from within that bleak cafeteria in the middle of a sandstorm I felt the pull of a real oasis.

Stepping back outside, I noticed that someone had washed the dust off of every light on my motorcycle. I found no one to thank. Ordinarily I might have taken that as a good sign, too, but I had no faith left for omens that day.

Judging from the map, Palmyra was at least as far away as I had just come, except the road no longer followed the river. It stretched through an unpopulated land. As I started up the bike, I still didn't know if I would carry on or find a hotel in the city. I threw a leg over, pulled in the clutch and kicked the bike into gear. Rolling along the gravel parking lot, weighing my options, I came to the highway. Finally the machine leaned left, southwest into the sand, toward Palmyra.

Visibility had improved and I could hold the bike almost straight up. Shadowy camels walked beside the road and I could see three or four dotted lines ahead of me. Off to the side I saw men with a cache of weapons. They had a heavy gun mounted to their truck, presumably used for patrolling the Iraqi border. The men watched me pass by. Then, just as suddenly as if someone had turned off a tap, the wind stopped.

I could see to the edge of the earth as the beige desert spread out to meet a watercolour sky. Wisps of cloud hung in the air like cigarette smoke and low hills rolled on the horizon. I lifted the visor for the first time that day to breathe in clean air. The sun was before me now, splintering off scratches in my sunglasses and casting a long shadow behind me.

My eyelids grew heavy and I felt myself slump forward onto the tank bag a bit. Pulling off the road onto the flat, hard surface of the land, I rode out about a mile until I came to a dry riverbed. I rode down into it. I switched off the bike. If only I had water. It was the wrong season for flash floods, so I could set up camp right there. No one could see me from the highway. But I had no water. I needed to reach Palmyra before nightfall. That was my last thought as I lay down in the shade of the motorcycle to sleep.

The next morning I awoke in Palmyra with just a blurry memory of how I got there. The sun was setting as I rode into town. I remembered taking a desperate drink of water and then dropping into bed, too tired to wash off the dust. I didn't sleep much. For most of the night I rocked forward onto my knees, kneeling in bed with my head on the pillow to keep from vomiting.

For several days I would remain sick and lethargic. Even so, when I woke in Palmyra that first morning, I was at peace. A call to prayer carried on the gentle breeze. I lay in bed listening to the muezzin sing his adhan. I smiled. This was it. At least for the moment, I had found my destination.

Jeremy Kroeker is the author of Motorcycle Therapy *and* Through Dust and Darkness.

Web: MotorcycleTherapy.com
Twitter: @Jeremy_Kroeker

Iran

Geoff Hill

The following is an excerpt from Way to Go, *published by Blackstaff Press (BlackStaffPress.com). Used with permission.*

In 1998, as the result of too many glasses of wine a few weeks earlier, Geoff Hill found himself in India with friend Patrick Minne, sitting on one of two Royal Enfields, just about to ride the 7,000 miles home to the UK. This was in spite of the fact that Geoff had previously only ridden 30 miles in his life (including 20 to the licensing test centre and back) and he and Patrick had been specifically warned by the British Foreign Office not to ride through Pakistan and Iran. Which is how, a couple of weeks later, they found themselves riding through Iran ....

The long road north from the Pakistan-Iran border was the sort of journey that would have been very dull in a car: 300 miles of desert and mountains with Mantovani on the stereo and whoever was in the passenger seat saying: "Heavens, Cyril, isn't nature exquisitely brutal!" But on a motorcycle, you're right there in the middle of it: the sun flayed us, fierce sandstorms poured salt on the wounds, desert rains cooled us, and the hot wind blew us dry. And through it all, the Enfields plugged away, God bless their little tappets.

When we weren't being toasted, sandpapered, soaked, and baked, there was little to do but appreciate what a Zen-like activity riding long distances on a motorcycle is, since, alone with your thoughts, there is plenty of time to contemplate the stillness at the centre of your being, which (as we all know) in traditional Buddhist thinking is one inch above your navel at a point called the hara. Which is, funnily enough, about the only part of you that remains still on a motorcycle like the Enfield, with its series of rhythms all designed to reduce your bones to marrow and your internal organs to jelly.

You see, whereas German bikes are built on the theory that, like the Third Reich, they will last a thousand years, old British bikes are constructed on the Zen principle that everything changes. At rest on an Enfield there is the slow heartbeat of that huge piston lolloping up and down; at cruising speed, a deep purr—like a lion after a particularly satisfying wildebeest—which slowly unscrews all the large nuts and bolts on the bike; and at high speed, there is a finer, more subtle threnody—like the wind in telegraph wires—which loosens all the small ones. Patrick would probably know a technical term for them all, but to me they sounded like the music of the stars.

Talking of which, after finally arriving in the ancient walled town of Bam, which is famous for its dates, we spent what remained of the evening discovering the amazing variety of solids that nine hours on a motorcycle in the desert leave up your nose. If some of mine had been asteroids heading for earth, they would have destroyed a city the size of Boston. Patrick, meanwhile, with commendable environmental foresight, was planning to take his home and use them as the basis for a rock garden.

After dealing with our noses, we dealt with our stomachs, eating dinner below one of the portraits of Ayatollah Khomeini that still hang everywhere in Iran, nine years after his death. To me he looked like Sean Connery, and I expected at any moment a voice to appear out of thin air, saying: "On shecond thoughts, better make that a double milkshake on the rocksh, Mish Mullahpenny."

How strange today was, I thought. I had expected it to be a monumental ordeal, but in fact it was one of the happiest days imaginable. Even the bad bits were good. The Buddha obviously knew what he was talking about when he said that if you expect nothing, everything is a gift.

It seemed remarkably unfair, however, in a country with no booze, to wake up the next morning with all the symptoms of a hangover. Still, it served me right for not drinking enough water the day before in the desert, so I downed a couple of litres over breakfast in Bam, while Patrick went off hunting for postcards to send to all his friends in Edinburgh, since "bam" apparently means something unmentionable in Scottish.

On the early morning road north to Kerman, I thought again about what it is that makes motorcycles so romantic. Perhaps it is because, if you think of old cowboy movies, the people inside the stagecoach or the train were always the passive victims of circumstance, whereas the lone figure on the horse was always the rescuer who did the good and necessary thing, then rode off into the sunset, a symbol of freedom and the nomadic spirit that the writer Bruce Chatwin thought was in us all, wanting to break away from the ties of settlement. Free of all that, the only relationship that lone figure has is with himself, whatever he happens to be sitting on and wherever he chooses to lay his head that night.

Think of all the solitary romantic figures that spring to mind—Jesus, Hamlet, Lawrence of Arabia, Dr. Zhivago, Charlie Brown. Indeed, sitting dusty, unshaven and saddle-sore at a rest stop in the desert with the snow-covered mountains in the distance, it was difficult not to feel like Clint Eastwood, the archetypal high-plains drifter. I wondered what he would have made of Iran, considering that both he and that other icon of late twentieth-century man, Father Jack, share the view that fine wine and fine women are probably the two most important things in life.

Here, the Iranians have banned one and wrapped the other up comprehensively in chadors, the all-enveloping black garments with, at times, only a narrow rectangle left for the eyes. Even in practical terms, it seems incomprehensible to wrap everyone up from head to foot in such a hot country. If you are going to have a Muslim nation, why not make it somewhere like Iceland? I'm sure it saves Iranian women a lot of time deciding what to wear every morning, but it's very disconcerting being surrounded by women cruising silently through the streets like Stealth pillar boxes with slots through which you feel you should post notes saying: "Is there anyone in there? Are you as hot as I am? Fancy going down the pub tonight?" But there's no point. The nearest pub is in Turkey.

Just before dusk, in the old bazaar of Kerman, swallows swooped above our heads in the endless blue of summer. And from all around, beneath the vaulted brickwork arches, drifted the aroma of a thousand spices and the ring of the metalworkers as they hammered out everything from exquisite jewellery with Koranic inscriptions so tiny they were almost invisible to copper tubs you could bathe the family in.

We were looking for a famous restaurant that had been recommended to us, but when we got there it was closed. Naturally. Outside the bazaar we found a man pushing an ancient Hillman Hunter, which were produced here under license in the Shah's days.

"You want taxi?" he said.

"Not if we have to push it," said Patrick.

"No, no, not at all," he said, jumping in and starting the engine, leaving it a mystery why he had been pushing it in the first place.

Back at the hotel, the television had been tuned to the Scotland v. Norway match in honour of Monsieur Minne living in Edinburgh. We gathered around to watch with the entire staff of the hotel; the chef was so engrossed that there was no possibility of dinner until after the final whistle.

We were joined by an American, who announced that his name was Trigger. Short for Happy, presumably. He had just come from Turkmenistan, where he had spent three days on the tenth floor of a hotel with no electricity or water, so waiting until the end of a football match for dinner was little hardship to him.

The Iranian TV coverage of the match, meanwhile, showed endless replays rather than crowd shots, in case the watching male populace would be whipped into a frenzy by the sight of an uncovered female elbow.

I'm afraid I have little time for societies which live in such fear of the naked human body, like Iran, Pakistan, and Ballymena.

The desert night was cold, and we slept wrapped in many blankets, then left early for police headquarters to have our visas extended. We still hadn't worked out why the Iranian embassy in London had asked us for a nine-day itinerary and then given us a five-day visa. It seems that this nonsensical behaviour is standard practice. The strange thing is that the Iranian people themselves are invariably as helpful, friendly, and happy-go-lucky as your average Dubliner. (I mean from the north side of Dublin, of course.) It is only when the veil of bureaucracy falls across their eyes that they become unseeing, unmoving, and unhelpful.

At the emigration office, the woman in charge—the first we had seen in any official position in Iran—told us we would need one photograph, a photocopy of the relevant passport pages and 10,000 rials (about £1.20). Great, we said. Could we get the photocopy and pay the money there and then? Of course not: that would have been too simple. We had to go to a photocopy shop around the corner, then lodge the money in a bank and get a receipt.

We did all this, and returned at nine.

"Thank you," she said. "Now come back at eleven."

Still, all this is nothing new. As Robert Byron said in *The Road to Oxiana*, published in 1937:

> The Persians have a talent for cutting off their nose to spite their face. They stopped the Junkers air service because it exhibited foreign superiority. They make roads, but their customs duties prohibit the importation of motors. They want a tourist traffic, but forbid photographs because someone once published a picture of an Iranian beggar, while conformity with their police regulations is a profession in itself.

* * *

Early the next morning, I visited the temple of Ateshkade in Yazd and found a fire of apricot wood burning in the centre of the room. Nothing remarkable about that, you may say, except that it has been burning since AD 450 as a symbol of purity and hope, kept alight by the Zoroastrians as they were bullied from pillar to post by all the bigger religions. It's hard to see why, since the basis of the religion is a relatively harmless belief that life is a constant struggle between good and evil, making it one of the easier faiths to follow, with only two rules: do good, and for God's sake don't let the fire go out. On the wall near the fire hung a portrait of Zoroaster (also known as Zarathustra), who founded the religion 6,000 years ago. He looked uncannily like Gene Wilder.

Apart from the temple, Yazd was made almost entirely of mud. Even the fourteenth-century mosque looked from a distance as if it was made out of mud, although closer inspection revealed it to be fine sandstone, while its tall, elegant minarets were veiled in a tracery of cobalt tiles as if they were attempting communion with the sky.

The taxi driver and I crept in as quietly as mice, while above our heads a colony of swallows flitted and darted below the vaulted dome. The driver spoke no English and I spoke no Farsi. We got on splendidly. At the mausoleum of Sayyed Ja'far, one of the line of holy men descended directly from Mohammed, the entire interior had been decorated in modern mirror tiles, and hundreds of women in black chadors were at their morning prayer.

I tiptoed out, returned to the hotel to find Monsieur Minne yawning and scratching himself, and we took the road north to Esfahan.

For the first two hours on a motorcycle in the morning, all the stiffness, aches and pains, and rattles in your body from the day before vibrate slowly all the way down and fall out through the soles of your boots, where they are collected later by the Iranian road service.

The second two hours are for cruising aimlessly along, with Patrick either half a mile ahead or half a mile behind, depending on whether he is revelling in the joys of Franco-Belgian mechanics or cursing the vagaries of Anglo-Indian motorcycle engineering. And the final two hours are for thinking about how sore your bum is, sitting on one buttock then the other to relieve the pain, and trying not to admit to yourself how much you're looking forward to finding a little hotel with a warm shower, a hot dinner, and a soft bed.

We arrived in Esfehan at dusk, and I fell in love with it immediately. If it was a woman, you would want to marry her. Well, unless you were a woman, in which case you would wish it was a man. Er, unless you were bisexual, in which case you wouldn't mind, or a priest, in which case you shouldn't care.

As Robert Byron said, unlike the Taj Mahal or the Alhambra, the beauty of Islamic architecture lies in form rather than decoration, and there is no finer expression of that truth than Esfahan.

"Before you know how, Esfahan has become indelible, has insinuated its image into that gallery of places which everyone privately treasures," was how he put it.

Arriving at a hotel recommended by the guidebook, we met someone coming out of the front door, muttering that it had the biggest cockroaches he had ever seen. Turning on our heels, we found another place around the corner, where the following morning, we were presented with a breakfast of egg and tomato puree masquerading as an omelette. Mind you, it was that kind of place: the room minibar was full of tinned peaches and the restaurant was only distinguished by a fine water list.

On our way to the Meldun-e-Emam, the 17th-century square, second in size only to Tiananmen and surrounded by some of the most beautiful buildings in the world, we were stopped by a small, dapper man called Iraj in an olive suit and black faux-crocodile loafers.

"Where are you from? Ireland? I have friends in Ireland," he said excitedly, producing a postcard of Dublin and then leading us down an alley into a subterranean teashop.

The walls were lined with carpets and swords and the vaulted ceiling was covered, above a dangling plethora of lamps, bells and a First World War German Pickelhaube, with sepia photographs of Iranian soccer heroes and wrestling champions with magnificent moustaches. In the centre was a photograph of Khomeini, looking suitably disapproving.

Beneath this vista of faded virility and quaint Edwardian charm, men sat all around at low tables drinking tea and smoking hookahs, both of which were duly brought and placed at our table, while Iraj produced photographs of travellers he had befriended on their way through Esfahan. Uncannily, we had met two of them, Marcus and Sonya, at the India–Pakistan border. He had also met Rupert and Andrew, the two Englishmen we had met in Quetta who were on their way to New Zealand. Iraj was obviously a full-time befriender.

We drank the pale, slightly acerbic tea and smoked the wild sweet tobacco, while from all around came the soothing hubble-bubble of the tall glass and walnut hookahs. It was very pleasant and soon I began to feel so light-headed and mellow that the only way not to fall asleep would have been to leap up and challenge one of the regulars to a hearty wrestling match.

Fortunately, at that stage we left and arrived at last in the square, where the Shahs once played polo and where the mosque of the Emam and the smaller mosque of Sheikh Lotfollah sit in contrapuntal harmony. They were, naturally, closed—in this case for Friday morning prayers—so we went to sit by the pool in the peaceful, exquisite gardens of the Temple of the Forty Columns, where Persian noblemen once welcomed foreign courtiers and then engaged them in languid orgies.

We stood for a long time outside the city's art museum, a building which is stunning in its simplicity, and returned to the mosques in the afternoon. Both astonish the European: Robert Byron remarked that he had no idea that abstract pattern was capable of so profound a splendour. The sense, both in the larger, more fabulous mosque and the smaller, simpler one, was one of immeasurably deep peace and contentment. Until the cantankerous caretaker threw us out, that is. Otherwise we could have sat there all day, watching the tiles change colour in the sunlight and moonlight. It was as if all the spiritual beauty in the world had been distilled into one drop, and its name was Esfahan.

We left, late in the day, for Qom, holy city of the mullahs. However, 100 yards down the road from our hotel, Patrick's bike spluttered and stopped.

As he got out the toolbox, we were surrounded within the space of a minute by every child in Esfahan, two village idiots who quickly became engaged in a punch-up (presumably over who was more idiotic), a schoolboy eager to practise his English, and a man claiming to be a mechanic. Fortunately, he actually was, and soon the problem was diagnosed as a dead battery, its terminals clogged up by sandstorms.

"Although I think you have some other electrical problem there," he said. "You should get it looked at."

We jump-started the Enfield, then around the corner saw a vision walking down the street: a young woman wearing a white wrap and orange trousers with blue polka dots. Heavens, the next thing would be a couple of mullahs calling around to see if we wanted to nip down to the Old Shah and Peasant for a few jars of best Tehran mild and a singsong. Even better, behind her we found a little hostel with a courtyard, a fountain, and four people sitting at a table playing multilingual poker. Dave and Jane were biking from England to Sydney to start a new life, and two Dutch girls, Martje and Jolanda, were making a documentary on the build-up to the Iran–USA World Cup game.

That evening, the holy night of Friday, all of us went for a walk down by the river, past picnicking families and the four beautiful bridges of Esfahan, until under the arches of the last we found a tearoom as festive and atmospheric as the inside of a Christmas tree, and sat on carpets in one of the arched windows with the river rushing by below.

Inside, the women were unspeakably daring. Some of them had flung their chadors back wantonly to reveal an earlobe, and one dazzling beauty wearing a white silk wrap draped decadently over her chador was flaunting both shamelessly.

Even more remarkable, the women here spoke to us.

"Do you not find this delicious?" said one sultry temptress, eyeing us coyly around the corner of a hanging carpet.

I wasn't sure if she meant the tea, the hookah, the almond biscuit I was foolishly holding halfway to my mouth, or herself, so I nodded anyway.

"Kheili khub (very good)," I said, since I'd been practising my Persian.

"Well done," she smiled sweetly.

I was in love, and not for the first time that day. Eventually we were getting on so well that the proprietor came over and told us to keep the noise down. I had just become Iran's first hookah hooligan.

Tragically, she left with her mother, but after a few minutes, Sultry Temptress II approached in a particularly fetching chador.

"Please take this seat," I said.

"Thank you, that's very kind. Do you like Esfahan?"

"Yes, you must be very proud of it."

"Why, no, I'm from Atlanta, Georgia," she said, popping her bubble gum.

We took a taxi home, the six of us and the driver in a Hillman Hunter, and at the hostel we ate apricots in the courtyard, while exotic people came and went silently on the surrounding balconies, like a production of *Othello* directed by Marcel Marceau. We fell asleep at two, the fountain tinkling outside the French windows of our little room.

If Monsieur Minne's motorcycle had not broken down, we would have met none of these people. Esfahan had blessed us twice, first by welcoming us, then by refusing to let us leave.

The next morning, Patrick spent half an hour cleaning his battery, kicked the Enfield into life, and declared himself satisfied. With a sweet sadness in our hearts, we climbed into the saddles and set off on the road for Qazvin: a road which we quickly discovered was not for the faint-hearted.

Iranian truck drivers, you see, see themselves as latter-day equivalents of German fighter pilots. Their enemy is anything coming in the opposite direction, and their favourite technique is lurking behind a slower truck then leaping out playfully as you approach, flashing their lights to indicate helpfully that your only alternative to death is to swerve into the quicksand that the Iranian road service habitually uses for verges.

"I'm fed up with this," announced Monsieur Minne at one water stop, after he had been forced off the road for the third time that morning. "I'm going to take them on at a game of chicken and see how brave they really are."

He lost one–nil, swerving aside at the last minute as the truck clipped the Enfield's wing mirror, then vanished in a cloud of dust.

We gave them the benefit of the doubt for the rest of the day, and just observed from a safe distance how, like fighter aces, they stencil their kills just below the cockpit, and decorate their vehicles gaily in the colours of their choice, with rakish symbols taken from a deck of cards, and religious slogans such as "Ya Allah" (Hurrah for God) or "Allah u Akbar" (God's a jolly good fellow), or romantic ones such as "Anjel" (sic) and "My Heart" beneath portraits of two unlikely *belle époque* virgins.

One truck which almost killed me that afternoon—I could not help but notice as I skidded into the quicksand and began to sink—bore the legend "Only You," beneath a painting of an Iranian siren who looked as if she was about to perform the Dance of the Seven Chadors, although you got the feeling that no matter how many she removed, there would always be one more, so that you would eventually die of frustration or boredom. In fact, in spite of the vision in polka dots and the earlobes incident, I had become increasingly convinced that, like nuns, Iranian women had no bodies, and that their heads simply floated along five and a half feet above the ground like hovercrafts, supported on an invisible cushion of spiritual wellbeing.

We could have done with a similar transport system ourselves, for the 300 miles north on the long road to Qazvin were dogged by fiddly, irritating problems, with tiny bolts consigning themselves willy-nilly to the wayside, and cables setting themselves free with gay abandon. Then at last there was one blessing: late in the afternoon, I finally passed the mystical 3,000-kilometre barrier on the odometer, which meant the bike was finally run in, and I could take the stabilizers off the back wheel and reach the giddy heights of 50 mph, a speed I had previously thought certain to cause blackouts due to lack of oxygen and the G-forces involved.

By early evening we had been eleven hours on the road and for the last two, as we raced north with the setting sun throwing a shawl of shadow over our shoulders, all I could think of was how sore my bum was and how much I was looking forward to a shower, dinner, and bed. But then the storm clouds that had been gathering over the lilac mountains disintegrated into lightning and re-formed into a rainbow, and the last rays of the sun lit the scene with a chiaroscuro Caravaggio would have given both arms to paint. As it were.

By dark, finally, we came to Qazvin, a pleasant, tree-lined town, which Byron said was noted for homosexuality and stupidity, although not necessarily at the same time. At our hotel, a vast building containing only us and the proprietor, the foyer was marble and the room glum. It would have been better the other way around.

Robert Byron had a better arrival in the town: "Stopping at Qazvin on the way back, I discovered the local white wine and bought the whole stock of the hotel. How comfortable that hotel seems now!"

I know what he meant. I slept fitfully on a reluctant mattress and dreamt of Tara Fitzgerald again. This time we were playing nude Twister, so you can imagine my disappointment when I woke up to find only Monsieur Minne, waking and scratching his hairy bits. Which are most of them, now that I think of it.

The people in Azerbayzan, as we crept ever closer to Turkey, were noticeably more European in their looks and manner. Mind you, they still had that quaintly charming and lethal Iranian habit of pulling up beside you on a moped or leaning out of a car window and engaging you in lengthy conversations just as you are arriving in a strange town and are in the middle of the life-or-death struggle to negotiate yet another anarchic roundabout. They usually cover topics such as where you are from, where you are going, what your name is, whether you are married, the state of your health and your considered opinion on Iran in general and their city in particular. "Hello, how are you?" is their universal greeting.

The landscape changes in northern Iran. All around us were fields of wheat and a colour that had been lost to our vocabulary: green. A rich, sap-filled green, alien to the parched south. And in the middle of this sea of fertility rises a sight as dramatic as Mont-Saint-Michel or the cathedral of Chartres—the gigantic, turquoise dome of Soltaniye, proof that the Mongol hordes of Genghis Khan were as nifty with a builder's trowel as they were with the sword. Built in 1313 by the Mongol Prince Oljeitu, it is, as Robert Byron said, the prototype of the Taj Mahal and a hundred other shrines, with the difference that it breathes power and contentment, while its offspring achieve only scenic refinement. Beside it is the dusty village of the same name, which in the fourteenth century was the greatest Mongol city of all.

I left Monsieur Minne snoozing by the bikes, and was shown around the shrine by a tiny woman in a chador, beneath the hem of which peeped a pair of exquisite Italian court shoes. In Esfahan we had seen entire wings of bazaars given over to shoes; they are about the only chance an Iranian woman has to express her individuality.

I returned to find Patrick in a state of scenic refinement himself, having his teeth inspected by the local dentist with an audience of every man and child in the village. On the dentist's desk tea was brewing on a spirit stove, while behind a shower curtain with an aquatic theme lurked a foot-powered drill and a rack of medieval instruments. Fortunately, they were not needed, and the only payment for the inspection was half an hour's amusement with the aid of useful expressions from the phrase-book, like *saghf tark khord* (the ceiling has cracked) and *Jasus nistam, zartoshti hastam* (I'm not a spy, I'm a Zoroastrian).

In the evening we descended through fields of lavender to the village of Miyane, found a little guesthouse, and sat down in the lobby that night with the entire male population to watch Iran play the USA in the World Cup. Iran won 2–1, the hotel proprietor celebrated grandiosely by buying everyone tea and biscuits, and for the rest of the night, cars drove up and down the street outside honking their horns. In Tehran, we were to hear later, young men and women danced and clapped illegally in the streets, scenes unprecedented in a country that has been governed since 1979 by men who never smile.

The next morning, the proprietor woke us at six and insisted on giving me an ad hoc tour of the hotel, including a rather impressive collection of Swedish toothbrushes which he had for sale. He then asked for payment of the bill. When I pointed out that we had paid it the previous night, he apologized profusely, demanded a tip, then woke us again at seven to ask when we were leaving.

To make matters worse, I had caught a cold. The temperature had dropped below 30 degrees and I wasn't a bit used to it.

The next day, in Miyane, I visited the family home of a young Iranian woman with whom I had had a wild fling in Belfast after we met in a flower shop and I invited her round for dinner, and with whom I had stayed in touch when she later moved to England. I spent that afternoon with her father, talking and eating apricots, which we picked from the tree beside the swimming pool. Beneath my slippered feet was an antique carpet worth much more than money.

It was a large and beautiful house, filled with sunlight and the memories of laughter. But they were only memories, because this was a family, like so many others in Iran, which had been split asunder by the revolution of the mullahs. I cannot even give the name of this charming and civilized man, and much as he would have liked to, he could not invite us to stay in his home for fear of repercussions, months of questioning, or even jail. He was careful throughout our conversation not to discuss politics. But then, he hardly needed to—virtually everyone else I had met in Iran was bitterly critical of the current regime and longed for the return of a liberal government.

Even when Ayatollah Khomeini returned to Iran in 1979, many of the Iranian middle classes had their doubts. There was a general feeling that the Shah had been foolishly persuaded by US arms merchants to squander the country's vast oil wealth on an enormous arsenal of weapons that would never be used. Many hoped that with the return of Khomeini, the country's wealth would stay in Iran for the good of the people. But it soon became clear that life under the mullahs was exactly like life in Northern Ireland would be under the Free Presbyterians—an endless wet Sunday in Portadown.

The Iranians must have known what they were letting themselves in for when Khomeini returned from exile in Paris to be met by scenes of hysterical adulation.

"What do you feel?" a reporter asked him when he stepped off the plane.

"Nothing," was the unsmiling response.

Of course, the present regime will come to an end, as all extreme societies do, whether decadent or puritanical. But in the meantime, all the people of Iran can do is count the long, wasted years. In this particu-lar family, the three teenage sons went to the United States, missing al-most certain death or injury as conscripts in the vicious Iran–Iraq war of 1980–88, which saw poison gas and wholesale slaughter in trenches for the first time since the First World War. Their mother followed to look af-ter them, and then their sister went too, unwilling to don the chador and with it a life of insufferable boredom without concerts, books, television, parties, dancing, or clapping.

Her father alone remained in that lovely house. There was no one to pick the apricots, laughter was only a memory, and the swimming pool was as empty as an ayatollah's heart.

Geoff Hill is the author of Way to Go, The Road to Gobblers Knob, Oz, *and most recently,* In Clancy's Boots.

Web: Geoff-Hill-Adventures.com
Twitter: @ghillster

Living is Risky

Mark Richardson

At the south end of Saugerties, N.Y, near the gas station, there's a larger-than-life photo of a young guy in a white shirt and jeans leaning against a tree. It's printed on vinyl on the side of a small truck parked beside the road. Its message is alongside in foot-high letters: "To My Brother, My Sisters, All My Friends, Family and Brit; Please Remember How Quickly Accidents Happen." Nothing else.

We stop for gas and when I go in to pay, I ask about the sign. "Oh, that was a young guy killed near here a couple of years ago," the attendant says. "Motorcycle accident, I think. His dad puts the sign out each summer. There's a benefit coming up for him soon." There's a small poster announcing the benefit on the local noticeboard inside the station; the poster has another photo of the young man alongside a picture of another guy. "That was his uncle. Killed while he was bush-hogging. A piece of the blade broke off and hit him in the head—real freaky." At the bottom of the notice is a phone number and I write it down, though I'm not sure why.

* * *

I ride on with Andrew, my 12-year-old son, into New York City. We follow Fifth Avenue all the way down to 57th, where I jog west below Central Park and then start making the turn south onto Broadway. At the last moment, a cop walks into the road and, with a raised hand, stops my turn—there's a crew setting up to paint the crosswalk. So I move back over into the lane to continue west, and at that moment, a silver BMW sedan with blacked-out windows brushes my right leg at high speed. It's so close I feel its bumper riffle my jeans.

That was close! Far, far too close!

The BMW speeds up ahead on 57th and dodges around another car that's pulling out of a side street. The driver's not slowing for anything. He's soon out of sight and gone. I ride carefully back to the hotel just a few blocks away. That really shook me up. Andrew doesn't say anything—it's clear he never noticed it, and I'm not about to tell him. I feel sick.

I park our Low Rider and we take the bags up to the room, which seems all the more dark and cramped for our day in the countryside. We hardly speak. Andrew changes and brushes his teeth and I leave him watching TV while I head down to the bar. That near-miss has me rattled. I take every precaution there is, but it's still not enough. In the back of my mind, I know if we'd been in a car we'd have been struck and bounced around, but would almost certainly have walked away unscathed, but on the motorcycle ….

There's a table open next to the sidewalk and I order a beer, thinking through the near-miss over and over, wondering what I should have done differently to better the odds. Be even more vigilant, I guess, but I'd checked over my shoulder before moving back into the lane and the BMW wasn't there. It was driving at probably 100 feet per second and just hadn't registered in my mirror.

Please Remember How Quickly Accidents Happen.

I can see the dead boy looking at me from the vinyl poster on the side of the truck. I take my notebook from my back pocket and open it to find the phone number I'd written down from the benefit poster, then pull out my cell phone and dial the number. I have no idea what to say. The person who answers is the dead boy's father.

* * *

Erich J. Rothe Jr. was 19 and working for his dad, Erich J. Sr., in the excavating business when he was killed two summers before. He'd ridden dirt bikes all his life on the family's 200-acre property outside of Saugerties, then moved on to road bikes once he was old enough—probably before he was old enough, if I'm reading properly between the lines of his father's story. When he was 18, he borrowed his dad's Harley Low Rider and went to Daytona Beach for Bike Week with his uncle. Apparently, there's a photograph of him, seen in his uncle's mirror riding behind, looking confident and like the King of the World. "I've never had so much fun with my clothes on!" he'd said at the time.

"I taught my kids to ride at a young age because I knew one day they would want to ride on the road and I wanted them to know what the hell they were doing," explains Erich Sr. "My boys raced motocross for a while. Erich had just bought a new pickup truck and he said to me, 'I'm going to buy a Jap bike.' I said, 'What the hell would you want to do that for?' He said, 'I can't afford a Harley right now with a truck on the road.' I said, 'Well, I don't want you to get a Jap bike—I'll help you get a Harley.' To be honest, I thought I was possibly saving his life, because them goddamn Jap bikes are just too fast. But that didn't work."

The two Erichs found a 2005 Low Rider very similar to my own, "a purple-pink kind of thing; from a different angle, it almost looked greenish-blue; we really didn't like it, but it kinda grew on you." On the morning of Thursday, July 26, Erich Jr. went up to Catskill and passed the test for his motorcycle license. That afternoon, he met up with his friend Zack after work. Zack was on his Kawasaki ZX-10, a monstrously fast sport bike. They must have looked like chalk and cheese: the Japanese racebike rider, hunched forward with his face hidden behind a full-coverage helmet, and the Harley cruiser rider, stretched out, wearing shades and a half-bucket.

"They were stopped at a stop sign, pulling out of a side road onto the two-lane. They were going to go to my house, but Erich said, 'Let's go for an ice-cream.' He had a smile from ear to ear, and he said, 'Let's ride!' That was the last thing he ever said. They only went a quarter-mile."

* * *

As it happens, Zack is there with some other guys visiting Erich Sr., and he takes the phone. Speaking about this, even to a faceless stranger, helps him to heal, he says.

"Every day that goes by, I think about it. It's the sound I think of—it's a sound I've never heard before. The impact was just so loud. I heard it over my bike and my bike was pretty loud because I was shifting gear. It happened so quick—I was looking down, then looked up and it was over."

Erich Sr. couldn't explain why his son was in the opposite lane when he crashed head-on into "a little Toyota, just a $500 piece of shit," but Zack knows full well his friend was riding too fast into a right-hand curve and drifted wide into the oncoming lane. The two were pegging their throttles—racing their bikes—and the Harley just wasn't designed for that kind of speed into that tight a corner. It was Erich Jr.'s bad luck that adrenaline got the better of him when another car was approaching. When they hit, he was thrown a dozen feet into the air and his helmet—loosely fastened, if it was fastened at all—flew off; when he landed, his head smacked the ground.

A car following the Toyota swerved when it struck the bike; it forced Zack off the road, but he dropped his motorcycle and ran over to hold his friend's hand on the asphalt. "I think he knew I was there because he wasn't breathing, but then I stood up and I started to cry and I said, 'My best friend is dead!' and then he gasped for a breath. His eyes were open, looking straight up. Every time I yelled, he gasped for air, but every time he gasped for air, blood would trickle out of his mouth."

Zack left his friend then. The ambulance was coming, and he rode his motorcycle to get Erich Sr., who lived just a few miles back along the twisting road. He tells me he rode like the wind.

* * *

Zack finishes his story and goes to find Erich Sr. to take back the phone. I feel stunned. I didn't know what to expect when I dialled the number, but I sure didn't expect this. Traffic on the street drives past. A car somewhere nearby jumps on the brakes and there's the sound of squealing tires and a horn. No thud, though. No impact.

* * *

"There wasn't a mark on his body, except for a perfect cross cut into his right cheek," recalls Erich Sr. of when he arrived and saw his boy. "It was like the man above put it there."

The paramedics were already at the accident scene, but they called for a helicopter and the father and son flew to hospital in Albany. For five days, doctors told Erich Sr. his son would make a full recovery. That all changed early in the morning of the sixth day. The teenager's brain had swelled and his brain stem was damaged. His heart pumped 180 beats a minute, struggling to feed the brain. A doctor walked in to give the blunt prognosis that "your son will never breathe on his own again." And that was that.

Four days later, the entire family gathered at the hospital. Erich Jr.'s mother, estranged from his father for 10 years, was there, as were his younger brother Willie and two younger sisters, one of whom had rushed back from vacation in Germany. Another 30 or so friends and relatives were also at the hospital, including his girlfriend Britney, who was at his bedside.

"The six of us were in there with Erich. His heart was beating out of his chest. I apologized to him for letting him die in a goddamn hospital bed, and I told him I couldn't stand to watch him there, so I told him I was going to leave him now and I left. Willie said goodbye too, and left with me. We went out to the big maple tree on the hospital lawn. For nine days, we'd felt so helpless—there was nothing I could have done for him. But then I turned to Willie and I said, 'There is one more thing we can do for him.' We went back inside and he was in the same situation and I looked at his mother and said, 'Enough is enough—let's end this nonsense,' and she said okay. And I turned to the nurse and said 'Let's turn this thing off, or whatever it is you do,' and she said, 'Okay, let me get a doctor.'

"It seemed like an hour but it was probably only four or five minutes and the nurse was back, and I said to her that 'I'll tell you one more time to go get that doctor and get his ass in here or I'm going to pull the plug on this thing myself.' He then came in, they gave Erich 10 mg of morphine and they just turned the dial down to slow the respirator right down. I just said my goodbyes, pretty much word for word what I'd said before, and I left. After everything we'd been through, I didn't want to watch him take his last breath—I didn't need to do that. Fifteen minutes later, my youngest daughter came out and said that he had passed. My youngest son carved Erich's initials and a cross into that big maple tree we were sitting under, and we went home."

Erich Sr., an excavator by trade, dug his son's grave with a backhoe at a small cemetery near the house. At the funeral, there was a procession of more than 200 motorcycles. Erich Sr. rode his new Electra Glide Ultra without his helmet in defiance of New York State's compulsory helmet law. Then after the service was over, he fired up the backhoe and filled in the grave himself.

* * *

We've been on the phone more than an hour—I hadn't expected to talk this long. I certainly hadn't expected a conversation like this. I'm thinking of all the responsibilities that a man takes on when he becomes a father and I realize Erich J. Rothe Sr. has been tested on every one of them. He encouraged his son to buy a motorcycle; he was there at his son's side on the road; he was with his son when he died.

"Erich was my best friend," says his dad. "Most parents can never say that, but we really could. This has just been so horrible that I still really can't believe it, but it helps me to talk about it. I just pray for you that nothing like this ever happens to you."

My cell phone battery is low, and after a few more minutes I thank him and say goodbye. He gave me an invitation to come up to Saugerties to fish on his property—that's his passion, fishing and hunting. His late son's, too. He set up a scholarship fund at Erich Jr.'s high school that awards bursaries of $1,000 each to students who excel both in their schoolwork and in outdoorsmanship; the upcoming benefit is to raise funds for that prize. The award is in the name of both his son and his brother, the man killed by the flying piece of metal while bush-hogging. That way, he told me, in a hundred years people will still remember their names. He could do with some of that money himself, though. He's worked just six weeks so far this year, and he's already behind a couple of payments on the mortgage. "I'll tell you, though," he said. "After what I've been through, there's a worse thing than being broke."

Erich Jr. doesn't have a gravestone yet—his dad is still trying to get together the money—though there's a giant stainless-steel cross donated by one of his friends in place beside the road at the accident scene. The truck with the vinyl poster that caught my attention is donated by another friend, and Erich Sr. said he put it there just before graduation, so maybe its message might help someone else. So some good could come from this tragedy, after all.

Zack remembers his friend with a tattoo: Erich had a German eagle etched into the skin over his rib cage and teased his friend that he wouldn't have the courage to submit to the needle, so Zack got himself an eagle over his ribs, with the letters EJR. And Erich's dad and his brother mounted a third mirror on their motorcycles. On that mirror, they've placed the photo of Erich Jr. riding behind his uncle in Florida, so he'll always ride with them.

* * *

When I get back to the room, I turn on the laptop under a small sphere of light above the tiny work desk. I'd asked Erich Sr. the name of the person driving the little Toyota that his son crashed into, and he told me it was a young guy named Darrin Francis. An accident like that must have affected him greatly, and I search for his name to see if I can find out more.

The name comes up quickly in a police report. Eleven months after the accident that killed Erich Rothe Jr., Darrin Francis was riding his Yamaha sport bike at 3 am northbound on the New York State Thruway with another motorcyclist. They lost sight of each other. He'd told that rider that he'd meet him at the Saugerties exit 25 miles away, but never arrived. According to a news report at the time, "After daybreak, state police patrols located the missing motorcycle off the right shoulder of the roadway, down an embankment in a small, barely visible marshy area. Francis's body was located close by, where he was pronounced dead by the Ulster County Coroner. State police state that excess speed and driver inexperience are probable contributing factors."

In bed now in the darkness, with Andrew sleeping safe next to me, five hundred miles from home, it's time to take stock of the situation. I feel I've been reminded of reality with a punch against the wall and a kick to the gut. The full weight of all my responsibilities as a father presses down. I've chosen to take my son away from his mother and brother on a vacation, and I've chosen to do it with a motorcycle, decried by many parents as far too dangerous to consider.

My wife and I went through all the questions months ago when this trip was first being planned seriously. She knows I'm careful on a motorcycle, and I've reminded her many times that I think of myself as safer on the bike than I am in the car, with less distractions and more focus. It wouldn't have helped us tonight, though. It sure didn't help Erich Jr. and Darrin.

But we're different, aren't we? I'm older—through the luck of the draw, I got away with my reckless behaviour and went on to learn from it and become more careful and more experienced. I always make sure Andrew and I are dressed properly, I double-check everything, and I slow right down. But how much of that leaves the motorcycle and crosses into our regular lives? As my son is about to enter his teens and launch headlong into his own Age of Reason, how much do I give, and how much do I take away?

I look over at him. There are no shadows on his face from the soft, dim light that comes through the window, for there's only a wall opposite our room, nothing moving in the night breeze to play games with my mind. I reach over and stroke his hair, then kiss the end of my finger and touch it against his nose. He doesn't move. His breathing is quiet and slow, and content. Complete trust.

* * *

A week later, in a hotel in Washington, I turn on the laptop and check the Internet connection. There's an e-mail message from a guy named Kevin. He read my note on MySpace a couple of days ago and wants to talk to me about his best friend, Darrin Francis. Here's my number, he says. Give me a call.

* * *

It doesn't take long into the phone conversation with Kevin before I realize he was the other motorcyclist riding with his friend on the highway that night. "Yes, it was me," says Kevin over the phone in Saugerties, as I listen from the couch in the hotel's hallway to his steady voice. "We did a lot together. We worked out together. We bought our bikes together. And a part of me died with Darrin on the highway."

They met, he tells me, when they were both working as aides at a nursing home near Saugerties, though only became friends after they'd both moved on. They were a couple of jokers: Kevin, part-Irish, part-Polish, part-Dominican; Darrin the black Grenadian from Brooklyn; but they were both ripped, body-building whenever they could. They worked as delivery drivers at the same pizzeria. In the summer of 2007, Darrin was 22 years old and had been out of high school for a few years, trained as a mechanic but not really doing anything with his life except partying, and not yet too concerned about it.

In the late afternoon of July 26 that year, Kevin and Darrin chatted for a few minutes on the street, then Darrin drove off in his old red Corolla to collect his next delivery at Riverside Pizza, which is just half a mile along the same highway from where Andrew and I had seen Erich J. Rothe's vinyl memorial banner on the side of the truck. Somebody out of town had ordered something to eat and Darrin set off to deliver it; minutes later, Erich and Zack decided to come into town for ice cream. Such a normal day.

"He called me then," remembers Kevin, his voice quite steady. "He said, 'There's been an accident—someone's run into me on a bike.' I thought he meant a bicycle, so I didn't really hurry over there. But when I got to the scene, the police were there and keeping us all back. The helicopter had already left with Erich. Zack was still there and I heard some of his comments about how the cops should check Darrin for drugs and stuff—he was obviously upset. Darrin had bruised up his arm so was staying in the car, which was a good idea." The driver's door of the Toyota was crushed shut by the impact and Darrin had to be helped out of the car through the passenger side, then was taken to hospital to have his arm checked out.

The two friends never really talked about the accident. Kevin says Darrin told him once that "I was just driving down the road and I thought, holy shit, he's coming over the line …"

The road is known for having patches of gravel scattered on its asphalt, and they thought perhaps Erich's bike might have slipped on some loose stones on the right-turning curve as he came up the small hill and over past the centre of the lane. Kevin also says Darrin wanted to go to Erich's wake, but cancelled at the last minute—he was worried he would be blamed for the death, but even more worried he would have the only black face in the room. Same thing for the funeral. So he just stayed away. He got on with his life, and even started dating Kevin's sister.

Later that year, when Kevin told him he wanted to get a motorcycle, he says Darrin showed no interest. "He said, 'You can get one, but I'm not going to kill myself,'" his friend recalls, and I hear a slight hesitation come into his voice. "But he came with me to Brooklyn in October to look at a bike and then he just turned to me and said, 'So—when are we getting mine, then?'" They didn't buy a bike that day, but sometime over the winter, Darrin went to his mother and asked for some money from his trust fund to buy some mechanic's tools, because he said he wanted to start working for himself. She gave him the money and in early May, he took $4,800 to Albany, where he paid cash for a second-hand Yamaha R6 sport bike, bought at auction and with an uncertain past. At the same place, Kevin found a Suzuki GSX-R 600 sport bike. The two motorcycles were well matched: small, light and very, very fast. Their riders were well matched, too: both had just beginners' licenses.

"His sister asked him why he'd bought a motorcycle after what had happened the last year, but he just shrugged. He was an easy-going guy. He didn't tell his mom. She and his dad live in Brooklyn, though they're separated, and when she came up to visit the weekend before, he had to hide the bike under a tarp."

"Before" means before June 29, 2008. In the early, dark hours of that morning, the two young men were riding home to Saugerties, heading north on the thruway from an evening at a bar in New Paltz. Kevin admits he'd had a few drinks; he won't comment on Darrin's state. "We'd taken off and he was a little behind me. I remember looking down at my speedo and I saw I was doing 95, so I slowed to maybe 75 so he could pass easily and he just blew right past me. He had this pipe on the bike that sounded like a jet fighter. I could still hear it after I lost sight of him."

Kevin sped up to catch Darrin but didn't see him, so he pulled off at the next exit in case he was there. He wasn't. Now Kevin was worried. He'd been riding so fast, he reasoned, that surely he would have caught up with Darrin. At the second exit in Saugerties, he asked the tollbooth operator if a bike had come through earlier, but says he already knew the answer. "The operator told me, 'I hope you find your friend.' So then I called my sister to see if he was there, and I wasn't really thinking about it, but one of the first things that came out of my mouth was, 'I think he crashed.'"

Kevin rode over to his sister's house then, and together with Darrin's nephew, who was staying over, the three of them drove in her car back down the 25 miles to New Paltz to scour the highway. But they could see nothing in the darkness, so they returned to Saugerties and called the cops. The police alerted officers on the thruway; they could also find nothing in the night.

Given the speed he'd been riding to catch his friend, Kevin figured Darrin must have gone off the road within three miles or so of entering the thruway at New Paltz, so once the dawn arrived, four of them, now including Kevin's ex-girlfriend, got back in the car, drove down to New Paltz and started returning north on the thruway. This time, they parked the car beside the road and got out to walk in the grassy ditch to look for evidence of the motorcycle. A police cruiser pulled up and the officer asked what they were doing; when they told him, he said he'd drive ahead and look for himself. Within five minutes, he called Kevin's cell phone. Reception was bad, so the phone didn't ring and instead, the officer left a stern message: "Listen, Kevin, when you get this, you give me a call. You get that? We found your friend." Kevin tells me he was crying when he drove to the scene a couple of miles up the thruway at a right-turning curve in the road, where the lone cruiser was parked on the hard shoulder. From the edge of the asphalt, he could see scattered bits and pieces of motorcycle in the ditch. The cop came up to the car and told everyone to stay inside.

"There were no skid marks," Kevin says. He pauses for a long time. "It's not that big a turn on the bike, but when I do it at speed in my car, I start to drift. I don't know if he went off the road just because he was going too fast, or maybe because there was something wrong with the bike. It was bought from an auction—it could have had issues we didn't know about. The sides of the bike were okay after the accident, but the front and back were wrecked. I think he hit the front brake and flipped it. He broke his neck and his back." Another long pause, then: "They say he died right away."

Darrin Francis had planned to go back to school and was already enrolled for the fall at a community college up in Hudson, NY, where he'd taken the mechanic's course; instead, his body was taken to a hospital, where his friends gathered in the hallway, together with his parents, up from Brooklyn. At one point, a nurse told them they could go upstairs to see the body if they wished and everybody clustered into the room. "He was still lying there with his helmet on, and with his clothes on that he had crashed in. He had blood on the helmet and some blood on his jacket sleeve, and then everybody went back downstairs and I think I just went home."

In fact, Kevin went back to work that afternoon, delivering pizzas. In the evening, a friend asked if he would take her to view the body, to say goodbye, and he did so. Darrin was still in the same room, lying as he'd lain earlier in the day, clothes and helmet still not removed, untouched. "The visor wasn't on the helmet, so I could see his face. I think his eyes were open a little bit. He didn't look like someone who'd been in an accident, not at all. I just couldn't believe it had happened. At least when I saw him with the helmet on and everything, he looked like I remembered. At the funeral, it really didn't look like him to me."

Darrin was taken from the hospital to the same funeral home in Saugerties that handled Erich Rothe's death eleven months before, and their visitations were held in the same building—the same room, even—just one winter apart.

I'm not quite sure what to say to Kevin. He's just telling the story of his friend over the phone to a stranger because he doesn't want the memory to go away, but I feel like a voyeur, curious about the details of the death. He tells me he sold his motorcycle: "I rode it once up to Albany—it just wasn't the same." He also says that on the week of Darrin's death, his friend was going to get a tattoo, but wouldn't say what it would be; afterwards, Kevin learned of the design and had it etched into his own skin on his left arm, the only tattoo he carries: God with a gavel, and the phrase "Only God can judge me."

* * *

Kevin mentions where to find some online photos and I write down the web address, and after the call ends, I go back to the hotel room. Andrew's writing in his diary about his day in the capital. I search for the photos and they come up quickly: a happy, confident, good-looking young man with friends, pictures taken at parties where there's plenty of liquor, faces of all colours, and action, action, action.

I sit still, staring at the snapshots on the screen. Very, very still. Behind me, I can hear the sound of Andrew's pencil sketching the sights of the day, scratching against the paper of his diary, recounting the story of his young life so far. The diary has many empty pages yet to fill.

Mark Richardson is the author of Zen and Now *and* Canada's Road.

Web: ZenAndNow.org
Twitter: @WheelsMark

No Politics for Lebanon's Hogs

Jeremy Kroeker

This article originally appeared in the Wheels *section of the* Toronto Star.

I skip from rock to rock holding my breath—as if that would help—because I know there are landmines in the region. At least there were. Before leaving the road and scrambling up the bank I asked my guide, Rafic, about that.

"They cleared all this land, right?" I said.

"Yes, they cleared it," he said. "Supposedly."

So I skip from rock to rock. I am looking for a vantage point from which to photograph a group of 40 motorcyclists against the backdrop of Lebanon's Beqaa Valley. The riders belong to the local Harley Owners Group (HOG) based in Beirut. They have invited me to join them on their weekly Sunday ride.

After snapping the photo, I take in the view. We are high in the Chouf Mountains near the Cedars of Barouk. Below us we can see the Litani River and, in the distance, snow-capped mountains near the Syrian border.

The land is beautiful, but it is also politically charged. The landmines attest to that. Here, the few mines that remain are throwbacks to the civil war of the 1980s. Just south of our position are thousands of cluster munitions, delivered by Israel during the 2006 war. Every swatch of land in Lebanon, it seems, is claimed by a religious sect and its representative political party.

Down on the pavement, I climb onto the back of Rafic's 2011 Harley-Davidson Ultra Classic. Like this, I can shout questions at Rafic as we snake along toward the valley floor. The road captains, all in orange vests, keep the group tight and organized. On this section, because of the sharp turns, they have us ride single file.

"This is where Lebanon grows all of its vegetables," shouts Rafic over the thumping engine noise. He points to the green valley. "They also grow a lot of marijuana here, too."

Rafic explains that Lebanon is so segregated into religious sects that he can tell where a person is from, sometimes even the very city or village, just by the person's name. By inference, he can also tell their religion.

"Where do most HOG members come from?" I ask.

"From all over Lebanon," says Rafic.

In other words, virtually every sect in Lebanon is represented within the group. I wonder aloud whether this creates tension, knowing that the man or woman riding with you is also a religious or political rival.

"Not at all," says Rafic. In addition to all the standard HOG rules—no alcohol, no drugs, etc.—the Lebanon Chapter does not tolerate any discussion of religion or politics. If a member begins to debate such topics at a HOG function, he or she is kicked out of the group.

"At the end of the day, we are just out here to have fun," says Rafic.

Back here in Beirut, that sentiment is reinforced by Carine, the assistant general manager of the newest Harley-Davidson dealership in the Middle East. She explains that, in Lebanon, the Harley brand is a unifying force. The manager of the dealership is a Shi'ite. Carine herself is a Christian, and most of the staff are Sunnis or Muslims from other sects. But that doesn't matter.

"It boils down to Harley-Davidson," says Carine.

"It's a beautiful story," she continues, leaning in for emphasis. Speaking about their well-attended HOG functions, she says, "It's the only time where we sit with a group of people and don't talk about politics or religion."

Jeremy Kroeker is the author of Motorcycle Therapy, *and* Through Dust and Darkness.

Web: MotorcycleTherapy.com
Twitter: @Jeremy_Kroeker

The Good Ship Chidambaram

Ted Simon

The following story is an excerpt from the book Riding High, *published by Jupitalia Productions (Jupitalia.com). Used with permission.*

In 1975 I arrived on the island of Penang in disgrace. The sense of disgrace was entirely in my own mind. I had ditched the woman I loved, causing us both considerable pain, because I felt the need to travel alone. My Triumph was crippled for the lack of a part which I had foolishly sent home weeks before in Singapore, thinking I would never need it. Then I went fishing and, as punishment for my sins, received a direct hit to my right eye with a lead sinker on the end of a ruptured nylon line.

In hospital, as I lay blindfolded in the hope that the retina would re-attach itself, someone stole all my documents from my bedside locker.

I came back eventually from these trials and tribulations, but it took six weeks before the dwarf stopped shining a light in the corner of my eye.

It wasn't until I loaded my bike onto the good ship Chidambaram and set sail for Madras that I finally felt whole again.

Chidambaram, Chidumbrrrum, how I loved to say ChiDUMbrrRUM—
the syllables resonating and reverberating between my lips.

The *Chidambaram* was a big white ship on a big blue sea, bound from
Penang across the Bay of Bengal to Madras, the last of the big ships for
me on my meandering trail around the globe.

For four days and three nights she would cosset me in careless indo-
lence before the great adventure of India, and the long ride home.

She was a fallen aristocrat. Once she had been called the *Pasteur*, when
she was a luxury liner on the North Atlantic route. In those days, she pan-
dered to wealthy gamblers who liked to while away their days and their
fortunes between Le Havre and New York at roulette and *chemin de fer*.

She still carried her haughty nose in the air. The large stairways and
lavish saloons were all intact, carpeted and embellished with engraved
glass and crystal, furnished with grand pianos and softly submissive so-
fas.

All this grandeur was devoted to a mere sprinkling of first-class passengers, and I was not strictly speaking one of them. In Singapore, when
I first inquired about the crossing, I was told that all Europeans were
obliged to travel first-class, lest they should find it too distasteful to share
cheaper accommodation with Indians. In Penang, however, the agent
confided that the policy was subject to mutation, and sold me a dormito-
ry berth, saving me a hundred dollars.

I soon found that my nationality and the colour of my skin were more
potent first-class credentials than any mere ticket, and I roamed the ship
at will.

At night I shared a cabin with three Indians and found nothing too
distasteful in that. Not even the cockroaches upset me. They were small,

black, and relatively unobtrusive. I ate spicy Indian food and liked it a lot better than the dull European meals served "upstairs," which I also sampled when visiting the *crème de la crème.*

Generally I spent the day observing the antics of the second-class Indians. Most of them seemed to be students going home from somewhere for the summer vacations. They were the noisiest and most aggressive people I had ever seen. To call them high-spirited would be like calling Hitler enthusiastic.

They devoted the larger part of their time to what they called "ragging." In the gangway outside my cabin I saw a miserable young man on his hands and knees surrounded by a yelling and jeering mob. He was fiddling with something on the carpet while behind him another man was making weird cranking motions with his arm, as though winding a starting handle. I found out that the victim was being forced to measure the length of the passage with half a matchstick.

"They are calling him a donkey and winding his tail," said one of my roommates. It went on for hours and sounded very nasty. The poor fellow was not as badly off as the Jews who were made to scrub streets with toothbrushes—at least at the end of the day he would survive—but I learned that, in India, ragging had often led to injuries and even death, and was forbidden by law. During the voyage, the purser several times broadcast warnings over the ship's PA system that ragging must stop and offenders would be punished.

The second-class bar was a scene of further enlightenment. It was strewn with empty beer cans, paper rubbish, and patches of vomit.

The barman glowered from behind a small hatch, part prisoner, part warder. He was a giant of a man, with a maniacal face deeply marked by fear, melancholy, and sheer hate. The patrons crowded around him like medieval bear baiters, taunting, prodding, and shouting demands. It was a bizarre and dreadful place that dealt another rude blow to my preconception of Indians as a courteous, soft-spoken people.

It was only on the second day that I discovered by chance the existence of a third class. With the thrill of descending into an ancient and unsuspected cellar, I found my way into what must once have been the ship's holds. I was amazed by what I saw. It was like being in a battery for hens, but with the cages enlarged to human proportions.

In these wire-mesh structures, large numbers of the very poorest Indians were bedded down with their belongings.

Their circumstances were probably not as bad as the impression they made. Ventilation was good and they could get out on to one of the forward decks. Their normal living conditions might well have been worse, but it was my first experience of seeing people organized into spaces and structures I associated only with domestic animals: India hit me there, for the first time, between the eyes.

The *Chidambaram* became my earliest crude model of Indian society. I saw her, in my mind's eye, sliced down the middle from stem to stern. In her hold beneath the sea, crammed into their cages as ballast, were the teeming masses, in an indistinguishable jumble of dhotis and saris, all contributing their iotas, which separately entitled them to their daily pittance of rice and dahl but collectively kept the whole ship afloat.

In the middle stratum a layer of loud, arrogant, bad-mannered men with their heads only just above water, wearing foreign clothes, speaking a foreign language, over-indulging in foreign habits, and pretending to a superiority that was in no way apparent.

And in the lofty upper reaches, occupying half the ship's accommodation, dwelled a handful of Olympian figures so far out of touch with the rest as to not even question their relevance; a few white-skinned transients and some light-skinned Parsee daughters from Bombay, wafting across the waves in pomp and splendour and acting out, all unwittingly perhaps, the undying traditions of the Raj.

On the morning of the third day I woke up early to hear unusual noises over the loudspeakers. Voices were delivering long messages, rather than announcements—I picked out words like "port" and "starboard"—and they were obviously meant for the crew. At the same time, I was aware of the ship making unfamiliar movements, and of other strange sounds outside the cabin. I pulled on my jeans, slid down from my upper bunk, and went out to look. A few yards along, where the gangway opened into an assembly point, a steel hatch in the side of the ship had been thrown open. It was about ten feet above sea level. A sailor wearing a life jacket and pajama pants ripped off at the knee stood at the edge, holding on by one hand. A rope ladder dangled beneath him and he was peering over the side with a troubled expression.

The first passenger to come by knew all about it.

"We are having man overboard. We are going back to rescue. This sailor is volunteering to jump in the water. He is being paid higher rate to do this."

I put on a shirt and went up to the lifeboat deck to watch. It was about half-past six. The sun was well above the horizon, the sky and the sea were blue and clear, and already there was a touch of heat. The ship was into the second half of the manoeuvre to bring her back to the point where the alarm had been given. There were plenty of people on deck, all Indians, including some officers in their white ducks, and they were eager to talk.

The man had gone over at dawn, from the third-class deck.

"Did he jump?" I asked.

"Nobody knows," said an officer. "But I tell you one thing. He was an old man, but when they threw out the lifebelts he swam to them like a champion."

"So he's all right?"

"Oh yes. Perfectly all right. We have put down the boat. Now we are going back to pick them up."

He smiled reassuringly. I had no reason to doubt him. The sea looked calm. The water was warm. I almost envied the old man in the sea his morning bathe, and I looked forward to his rescue as a harmless but interesting demonstration of something I had never seen done before.

The lifeboat was easy to spot, but as we drew closer its behaviour seemed odd. It was floating, but going nowhere, and bobbing up and down in a way that made me realize there was more of a swell than I had thought. There were three men on it that I could see. They had oars out, but the boat was so high in the water that the blades hardly touched the surface. As I watched, the crew appeared to give up rowing and pulled in their oars. Then I caught sight of the old man. He had his arms through two bright red lifebelts, and was floating some way away from the boat.

The officer was still standing nearby, smiling equably at my questions.

"The propeller of the lifeboat has been damaged," he told me, "but we will soon get him out."

The ship drew nearer to the old man, and I saw him plainly. Only his head and naked shoulders were above water. He was a well-built, quite striking figure, with skin the colour of a hazelnut, a completely bald head and a pair of bushy white whiskers. The most extraordinary thing about him, though, was his absolute immobility. The ship came within thirty yards of him—I could have ringed him with a quoit—but he never raised his head nor let a flicker of emotion change his expression, which was one of total resignation as he floated by, more like a waxwork effigy than a man.

I watched this with great surprise, feeling sure that in his position I would have had to laugh or shout or, at least, acknowledge the hundreds of spectators gazing down at me.

Then we were past and leaving him behind.

"Why aren't they going for him?'" I asked indignantly, thinking of the volunteer sailors waiting to swim for their money. "Why don't they get a line out?"

Every new episode in this affair astonished me. A passenger leaning over the rail shouted excitedly in his own language, pointing down. Whether he had heard my question or not, he provided the answer. Below us, beautifully visible in every detail and circling lazily beside the ship's hull was a shark. It was eight feet long or more, dark brown in colour shading to white at the tips of its fins, an elegant and menacing fish.

People all around were calling out now.

"Look, look, shark! Oh dear! White-finned shark. Most dangerous …" and so on.

A juddering vibration ran through the ship as the propellers went into reverse. The loudspeakers began to bark.

"… Number three lifeboat," I heard.

The derricks rattled and another boat, with several men inside, swung out over the side on the two cables and slowly descended.

What then followed was a scene of danger and violence I would never forget. Perhaps because the ship was now almost at a standstill, she began to roll a little more with the swell of the sea.

Though it was not a movement that was even vaguely uncomfortable, it was enough to start the lifeboat swinging on its cables, and before it was even halfway to the sea it had begun to smash against the side of the ship.

The first collision was mild, the second much harder. The third was an almighty crash. The men in the boat were flung down and the side of the boat buckled. Its descent into the sea seemed painfully slow, and it received several more tremendous blows before its keel was in the water. I could see now what had disabled the first boat, and it was a wonder to me that this one had survived. In all the times that I had heard or read about "lowering the boats" from stricken liners or torpedoed warships, I had never imagined anything like this.

Now the lifeboat was in the sea but still attached at bow and stern to the cables. These ran through huge steel blocks, or pulleys, with shackles attached. The blocks could not have weighed less than a hundred pounds. One of the crew was trying to unfasten one of the shackles. It was clearly hard to do and took him several minutes.

Then his end of the boat was free and floating with its full weight on the water, while the block swung loose on its cable. The other end of the boat, however, was still attached, and the result was practically lethal. The free end bobbed up and down on the waves and threw the boat into wild motion, making it almost impossible to unfasten the other shackle. Meanwhile, the free block began to swing across the boat with irresistible and deadly momentum, knocking the sailors down and narrowly missing several skulls.

Their frantic efforts to release the second shackle finally succeeded, and the boat at last got away. Miraculously, its engine and propeller were intact, and it made off to find the old man, whom I was expecting, at any moment, to see pulled down beneath the surface by a devouring shark. It took the crew a long time to haul him in. By now he had been in the water for more than an hour. Then the boat went on to collect the lifebelts that had been thrown after him before coming back to the ship on the port side. But the swell prevented the crew from making fast, and they were sent off again to find the first, damaged lifeboat and tow it back to the ship.

The boats moved very slowly. It was almost an hour later that everything was assembled at the ship's side, but there was still another minor surprise waiting. Instead of taking the old man up in the boat with the crew, they decided to haul him in through a hatch.

To do this, he was wrapped in a canvas shroud, like an Egyptian mummy, and drawn up by a cable on pulleys, a bosun's bed, as it were. Why this was done I never knew. I would swear that he was alive when we first floated past him, and I saw his face again, framed by the canvas as they dragged him in, as much a graven image as ever. It did not occur to me until much later that he might have died.

The excruciating business of lowering the boats was then repeated, twice, in reverse. Exactly the same dreadful pendulum swinging inexorably over the crew as they ducked in terror, and the same fearful crunches against the side of the ship. The men stood hanging onto the cables for dear life. An officer on deck shouted at them, again and again: "Sit down. SIT DOWN," but they were beyond even hearing him. Then the boats came inboard and it was all over.

The same officer I had spoken to earlier was back again, looking as pleased with life as ever. I asked him why there had been so many problems.

"Ah, it was the heavy swell, you see," he said. "It is a simple matter."

"Every two weeks we practice putting the boats in the water. Just some weeks back our radio-op jumped overboard. We had him out again in eleven minutes."

Eleven was a propitious number. I suggested that it might all have been a lot easier if the blocks and shackles had gone down a lot faster and farther than they did.

"Yes," he said, as though agreeing with me. "They go down quickly under their own weight."

It was so obvious that they did not, that I stood nonplussed.

"Was anyone hurt?" I asked, feeling sure there must have been some bones broken.

"No," he replied, happily.

Two minutes later someone came by to comment that there were several men in the ship's hospital with serious injuries.

"Yes," agreed the officer, just as happily. "You see, if the boat had been full of passengers it would have been quite different, because of the extra weight. And also the passengers are asked to cooperate by moving to this side and that."

"But if you can't get your own men to take orders, why should hysterical passengers listen to you?" I asked.

"Yes," he said, "The passengers will certainly do as they are told. They will know it is best for them."

He rocked his head from side to side in that delightful, liquid movement which signifies not mere assent and agreement, but complete acceptance of the ineffable goodness of things as they are.

The excitement subsided and life returned to normal as the ship resumed its course. Stimulated by the long drama, I became sharply aware of how strong and optimistic I felt. Every aspect of life was full of meaning. The depression that had ground me down in Penang was gone. Not a trace of it remained. I looked down over the ship's side. The shark had gone, too. The sea looked as peaceful and lovely as ever. The big white ship gathered speed and sailed on over the beautiful blue water to Madras. Soon it became hard to believe that there had been any kind of unpleasantness at all.

Raised in London by a German mother and a Romanian father, Ted Simon found himself impelled by an insatiable desire to explore the world. It led him to abandon an early career in chemical engineering to go to Paris, where he fell into journalism.

On 6th October 1973, at the age of 42, Ted set off from London on a 500cc Triumph Tiger motorcycle on what became a four-year solo journey around the world, covering 64,000 miles through 45 countries.

With the aim of discovering how the world had changed in the intervening 28 years, on 27th January 2001, aged 69, Ted embarked on a second journey. This time he rode a BMW R80 GS over 59,000 miles through 47 countries.

Ted's books about his journeys, Jupiter's Travels, Riding High, *and* Dreaming of Jupiter *continue to serve as an inspiration to other travellers who seek to know the world, and their place in it, through personal adventure.*

Web: Jupitalia.com

Web: JupitersTravellers.org

Young, Wild, and Riding Free

Natalie Ellis Barros

You might say it was a little metaphorical that my first solo adventure on a motorcycle would be heading six hundred miles down the "One" to pick up my college diploma. I was too cheap to pay the sixty dollars for it to be mailed and I needed my first real ride, alone. So, closing one chapter of my life and riding straight into the next, I heaved myself and a bunch of gear onto the back of my beautiful GS and hit the road for Southern California.

I know it's not around the world or anything, but after three hours of mingling with commuters headed to the Bay Area on the I-680, bending against the ocean breeze and squinting into the glare of the sun off the iridescent waters, I felt like I was in a magical place. The wind tries to topple you on that section of the 101, just when you can see the ocean but haven't hit Monterrey yet. I wanted to go faster than 70 mph because the road just sits there open and clear, and the sun smiles down, but the wind wants nothing more than to throw you off your bike. And all my "23-year-old-on-her-first-adventure-ride" gear was strapped on so poorly that it acted in concert with the wind, trying to knock me over every chance it got.

It was in that moment, when all the muscles in my tiny body were tightened together to keep up the bike—I occasionally had to punch the bags behind me to straighten them out—that I started crying. But the tears weren't born of some "girly" frustration or weakness; they flowed from the pure happiness and thrill of being alive that only motorcyclists can understand. Of course, soon the foggy-eyes business began to impair my vision, so I opened my visor to dry off, laughing aloud at the whole scenario as I blew past a VW van loaded with surfboards.

I stopped in Monterrey for a late lunch at a lovely American diner just off Cannery Row. There were red Naugahyde booths to throw my gear upon, and a menu so fatty and burger-filled it was guaranteed to strain the heart. It also had the best fish tacos I've ever tasted.

As soon as I took off my helmet, on came the stares and the questions. Being a strong advocate of "All the Gear, All the Time," I can appear genderless with my helmet on, which can come in handy if I'm filling up the tank in a sketchy place. But once I expose my feminine locks and features, the reaction of onlookers changes (so far as I have experienced) in a surprisingly positive way.

As a woman, I've been objectified and harassed by men frequently. It seems that no matter what I'm wearing, be it sweatpants or dance clothes, a cocktail dress or a parka, there's always someone who feels the need to be crass or send his hungry eyes my way. But every man I've encountered while I'm in my bike gear has treated me only with the utmost respect and admiration. They often ask me questions about my journey and my bike, but always encourage my independent nature. In fact, it's usually women who either glare in disapproval, ask me why I'm "inviting danger," or simply refuse to acknowledge me. It seems to me, more and more, that it is women who put our gender in a box, rather than men.

Returning to my journey, the smooth pavement continued as I headed farther down the warm coastal highway. Unfortunately, it was clogged with more traffic than I'd expected on a weekday in the middle of November. It wasn't so much that there were a lot of cars (as there might be in the middle of summer in California), but that there was always a tourist in a rental car creeping around the one-lane curves. No matter how many I passed, there was always another caged creeper just down the road, forcing me to turn my focus from speed to scenery.

I might have thanked the pokey tourists for that opportunity to stare at the sea if the camping spot that I had planned on stopping at hadn't been full, making time an issue. The sun was setting and it was starting to get cold. I had passed Big Sur and was going to have to start racing the clock. I had thrown around the idea of just stopping somewhere on the road and attempting to lay out my sleeping bag in some brush in the hopes of going unnoticed. Then again, the idea of being woken up by a cop—or worse—in the dead of the night kept that idea as a last resort.

The sun had gone down about an hour ago. I was exhausted and knew that I was entering the "danger zone" (and, no, not the fun Kenny Loggins one). The more I continued down the road, the more dangerous I became to myself and to others. "Cambria 6 miles," a road sign said, and I pulled off into what I thought was Cambria some time after that, looking for answers. My phone was almost dead. I had it in airplane mode to save energy, but with or without it, I felt utterly lost.

I hadn't seen a campground on the map after Big Sur until San Louis Obispo, and I was stuck in the cold some hundred miles or so in between. There were a few hotels, but this was my only night on the road before heading into to LA tomorrow, and I refused to give in and stay in one.

Not only was I pretty broke, being a recent college grad, but I knew that I would have felt like an utter failure. I had ridden all this way, with all this crap on the back of my bike, to prove to myself that I was independent and strong. I had done this to prove that I had grown from Mom and Dad's little college girl into "adventure woman," ready to embrace the world with nothing but a F650GS and a tent. And now I was supposed to just call it quits and pitch up in a hotel?! Hell no! I took a deep breath, latched my helmet back on, straddled "Lady Godiva" once again and took off south. Sure enough, about a mile down the road, I found my deliverance from the winding One: San Simeon State Park. Apparently I hadn't hit Cambria like I thought I had.

The little brown sign with the shiny triangle tent icon glowed in the night, and I took a solid breath of relief. I followed the dirt road on my trusty dual-sport—I had told my friends that this option would come in handy!—up the hill towards the inaptly-named "primitive" camping sites. It was dark but I found my way around, and my spot of choice had a nice picnic table and grill. I pitched my tent in under ten minutes and decided I'd leave the fly off because I wanted to wake up with the sun, since my phone was now dead and I had no alarm. Terrible idea. Even though it wasn't as cold as one might expect on a northern coast in November, it was still cold enough for me to wish I had put the fly on and woken up whenever the hell my body wanted to. Nevertheless, it was a lovely night. I was freezing, but I had the luminescent full moon and howling coyotes for company.

No sleep and no warmth didn't mean I had no reason to smile. Sure I was frightened—who knew what was out there waiting to prey on a woman alone, with nothing but a bit of pepper spray and a pocket knife clutched to her chest for defense?—but then again, when had I ever felt this? On my own, wherever the road would take me, on the most wonderful vehicle for adventure that humankind has ever invented? This is what I had wanted out of life. So many of my friends and peers were struggling to figure out what they wanted. Thrown into the "real world," they wished they were back under the security blanket of student loans and grade point averages to define who they were. I didn't want to go back—well, besides to pick up my diploma. I didn't want to be anywhere else but on the road.

I woke up with the sun after sleeping only a handful of hours, packed up in under 30 minutes—this time making sure my packing was a little less ... dynamic—and hit the road. I passed what was actually Cambria with the sun in my eyes and saw Morro Bay for the first time shortly after that. I've lived in California for the majority of my life and have been up and down it a dozen times, and I'm still finding places I never knew existed. It was a quiet and fresh morning and there sat Morro Rock, tall and magnificent, a soldier in parade position waiting at the ends of the Earth for me to pass her and salute.

I stopped for breakfast in San Luis Obispo and discovered that it was about 7:30 am. I continued on along the coast to Santa Barbara and decided I'd take the 101 into LA to visit some people before heading down to Newport Beach, where my best friend was waiting to celebrate the weekend with me.

By 2 pm, Hollywood was already hell. I knew I hated driving there, but riding with too much gear to split lanes and risk denting a Maserati was even worse. Luckily, a good friend of mine lives a block away from the Chinese Theatre. So I parked the bike and locked up my gear at his place, and he and I took to the streets. We laughed at the tourists, judged the hipsters, and admired the Art Deco that hides behind the superfluous glamour of modern Hollywood.

I spent the weekend in Newport Beach, my old stomping ground, and finally picked up my diploma from UC Irvine just before heading back up Highway 1 the following week. I had never gone up past Long Beach on the Pacific Coast Highway, so up I went with what seemed like a lot more courage and self-assurance than I had come down with. My gear never wavered and I pissed off countless drivers stuck behind each other as I fearlessly—but cautiously—scooted between them and past that vast and crowded city.

I took my time on the way up, stopping at "points of historical interest," and points that I thought were interesting even if no one else did. I stopped at an abandoned well stuck in the side of one of the many curves of the road, as well as a tree that hung to the ground like a stooping old woman. I even went out of the way to visit the Inez mission that sits just past the way-too-adorable town of Solvang that I just couldn't bear to stop and take a photo of. I camped again on the way up and this time I remembered to charge my phone so that I could throw up the fly. Nevertheless, it died as soon as my alarm went off, so I never really got any photos of the campsite. Maybe next time I'll invest in a real camera.

I hit the road early in the morning and got to see elephant seals playing on the beach before the tourists swarmed them with camera lenses. My gas light went on and I had to wait at the gas station in Ragged Point for the place to open and my phone to charge. At $5 a gallon, I felt, once again, blessed to be riding a motorcycle and not some gas guzzler.

When I took off again, it was just after 8 am and the road was empty.

I slowed down to keep pace with a red-tailed hawk. At first, he nearly crashed right into me, but then for almost a whole mile he flew beside me. He was close enough that I could make out the sharp curve of his beak and the bright red of his tail feathers. I smiled from under my helmet, and when my companion finally took off and I went around a bend, I knew I could never feel more alive. I've never believed in fate but, if there is such a thing, then this is it. This is what I was meant for.

I startled a bobcat that scampered uphill like a bullet, and I slipped past the ever-crowded Big Sur seemingly unnoticed. I stopped for lunch in Monterrey again and, as I turned inland, I sang Prince at the top of my lungs. The beauty of the full-faced helmet is that you can still look like a bad-ass while screeching "Little Red Corvette" at the top of your lungs. When I finally did arrive home, I was more exhausted and more fulfilled than I had ever been in my entire 23 years of life.

Next stop, South America. Anyone down?

Natalie Ellis Barros is a professional dancer in the San Francisco Bay area with a "Ride-or-Die" attitude and the tattoos to prove it. Follow her on Facebook, and on Instagram @Natalie2gogo.

Afterword

Jeremy Kroeker

At the end of every book project, I silently promise myself that I'll never do *that* again. "But of course," as Ted Bishop put it in his contribution to this anthology, "the only way I get anywhere interesting is through willful self-delusion—an essential character trait for both motorcyclists and writers."

Indeed.

And that's a wonderful character trait, isn't it? Almost all of the writers in this book have happily deluded themselves to one degree or another, and it lead to adventure. Yes, underestimating risk can be dangerous, as Jordan and Sandra discovered in Guatemala, but overestimating risk is often worse—it could mean that you never leave home.

What a tragedy that would be, if none of us ventured into the wider world to seek connection and understanding. Ted Simon might never have left England in 1973, at the age of 42, if he succumbed to the fear that taking his journey would forever cast him to the outer circles of society, always looking in on the lives of the comfortably secure people. He struggled with mortal fears and self-doubt in the pages of his seminal book, *Jupiter's Travels,* and aren't you glad he did?

He came back from his adventure with an understanding that, essentially, people are good and kind, and that the more vulnerable a person becomes while travelling, the more hospitable a place the world can seem.

That's where the motorcycle comes into play. We are exposed on these wonderful machines. We are fragile. And we are usually better off because of it.

If there is a theme in this book, that's it. It happened by accident, just falling into place like most things do while on the road.

There was, however, a bit of thought put into the order of the collection. It begins with a foreword by Ted Simon, then stories by Lois Pryce, Ted Bishop, Mark Richardson, Carla King, and a few others. These are the "old guard," so to speak, the veterans of motorcycle travel writing, the ones we venerate and quote while gathered around the campfire. But the book ends with a story from a young Ted Simon, written decades ago, followed by the youngest contributor, Natalie Ellis Barros. Her story was chosen to close out the anthology based not on the merit of the adventure itself, but on its energy.

I love it. She's calling us out. Let's keep taking risks. Let's ride. Let's travel. Let's delude ourselves, just a bit.

You know, maybe it's about time I hit the road again. Or maybe I'll start writing another book.

Alberta, Canada
2015

Acknowledgements

First I need to thank all the contributors to this anthology. Thank you for your hard work, your rewrites, and your patience with me as I muddled through the process of making this book a reality. To single out just a few, Sam Manicom encouraged me early in the process, and he was one of the first to send in his copy … way ahead of deadline.

Speaking of deadlines, Mark Richardson taught me that editors must never extend them because the writer will just use that extra time to drink beer.

Thanks to Don Gorman, publisher at Rocky Mountain Books (RMBooks.com), for lending his support and advice. Don took a chance on my second book, *Through Dust and Darkness,* and I remain grateful for that, as well.

Imaginary Mountain Surveyors (ImaginaryMountains.com), publishers of mountain fiction, gave of their time and expertise. Jerry Auld at IMS did the layout in addition to offering up coffee and commiseration.

I need to mention, and thank, The Ted Simon Foundation (JupitersTravellers.org). Many contributors to this book are involved with this non-profit organization in some way, either as advisors, travellers, or just enthusiasts. The foundation believes in the power of stories, and it aims to help riders and travellers tell those stories to best of their ability.

Scott Manktelow was dragged out of retirement to design the cover. Jennifer Groundwater did much of the heavy lifting on the writing with her thoughtful edits and multiple readings of the manuscript. If problems remain in the text, I take responsibility for that. Sometimes I break things that others have struggled to make beautiful.

Nevil Stow makes a mean garagarita, and his lovely wife, Michelle, puts up with our caterwauling after we've had a few. Their daughter, Jessica, just shakes her head. More often than not, Issa and Nita Briebish are in on the scene, but they actually sound OK.

Listing a vast amount of people is dangerous, because someone always gets left out. And those that are mentioned wonder, "Why did he just slot me into a stupid list?" But I'm doing it anyway. You people matter, and those of you that I left out are even more important.

So, thank you Matt Jackson (of Summit Studios), Iain Harper, Paddy Tyson, Leighton Poidevin, Heath McCroy, Lynda Gale, Deborah Lantz, Beth Frizzell, Dave Coe, Bryan Bayley, Jocey Asnong, Joy Maclean (and the entire staff of Café Books in Canmore), Kristy Davison, Greg Bouk, Nika Hubert, Dave Anderson, Mary Laird (at Toad Rock Campground), Angie Abdou, Andrew Querner, Grant and Susan Johnson (of HorizonsUnlimited.com), Brent Peters, Flip Morton, Paul H. Smith, Allan Karl, Rene Cormier, Dustin Lynx, Ekke and Audrey Kok.

Ok, that's a slippery slope. I want to thank all the Horizons Unlimited crew that I see every summer in British Columbia, and every fall in California. Thanks to the Garagarita crew, and more. But I can't list you all. You know who you are and, copout though it may be, I do appreciate you. See? Long lists are dangerous.

Finally, although he's been mentioned a lot already, I want to thank Ted Simon. You've inspired us all.

How about you? Are you a Motorcycle Messenger?

If you have a true, interesting tale from your motorcycle travels, we'd love to read it. You don't have to be a professional writer for us to consider your work, but you should take the craft of writing seriously. We'd rather have a well-written story about your trip to the corner store than a poorly written yarn about how you flatted out in the Ural Mountains and survived a bear attack. (Although, we'd definitely like to read that story, too.)

For more detailed submission guidelines, please contact us at **OscillatorPress.com**.

Also by Oscillator Press:

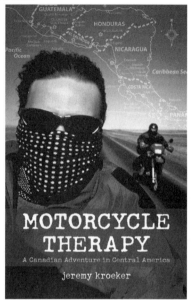

From the Canadian Rockies to Panamanian jungle, Motorcycle Therapy rumbles with comic adventure as two men, fleeing failed relationships, test the limits of their motorcycles and their friendship. Join the horn-honking, signal-flashing, wheelie-popping pair as they endure painful bee stings, painful snakebites and (when they talk to girls) painful humiliation. Even if you hate reading, motorcycles and travel books, you'll love reading this motorcycle travel book.

"With humour that's reminiscent of Bill Bryson's best, Kroeker discovers that you can't leave yourself behind—but it's sure fun trying."

Chris Scott, author of *Adventure Motorcycling Handbook*.

Also by Jeremy Kroeker. Published by Rocky Mountain Books.

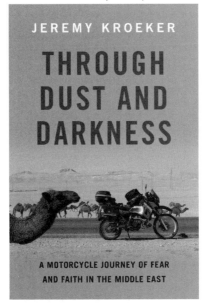

JEREMY KROEKER is a Mennonite with a motorcycle. When his seemingly unflinching faith in a Christian worldview begins to shift, he hops on his bike to seek answers. After shipping his ride to Europe, Kroeker discovers that the machine wobbles worse than his own opinions about spirituality. Still, he caries on, oscillating through Germany, Austria, Croatia, Albania, and into the Middle East: Turkey, Syria, Lebanon and, ultimately the theocratic nation of Iran.

It is there that Kroeker takes a forbidden visit to a holy Muslim Shrine. Once inside, invisible hands rip from his heart a sincere prayer, his first in many years. And God hears that prayer. For before Kroeker can escape Iran, God steals into his hotel room one night to threaten him with death. At least, that's one way to look at it.

Oscillator Press thanks the following corporate sponsors for helping to make this project a success:

MotoStays.com is a home sharing network specifically for motorcyclists. Our mission is to enhance your travel experience through accommodation alternatives. Spend less, experience more!

Web: MotoStays.com
Email: info@motostays.com
Twitter: @MotoStays
Phone: 720.841.3009
Locations:
          Worldwide
          (28 countries & counting)

Aside from riding a motorbike, Banff Airporter is the best way to get between Calgary Airport and Banff, Alberta. Enjoy the convenience of frequent schedules and modern vehicles.

Web: BanffAirporter.com
Email: info@banffairporter.com
Twitter: @BanffAirporter
Phone: 1.888.449.2901

Blue Circle Insurance: We are Alberta's leader in motorcycle insurance, but specialize in home, auto and commercial too. We are a referral-only brokerage, so we must be doing something right!

Web: GoBlueCircle.com
Email: insurance@gobluecircle.com
Phone: 403.770.4949
Location:
          200, 3402 8 Street SE
          Calgary, Alberta T2G 5S7

OVERLAND Magazine, the quality international quarterly dedicated to motorcycle travel, contains captivating stories and stunning photography to inspire, enthuse and entertain.

Web: OverlandMag.com
Email1:   editor@overlandmag.com
Email2:   sales@overlandmag.com
Location:
           Overland Magazine
           Riverside Works
           Cropredy
           Oxfordshire
           OX17 1PQ
           United Kingdom

Oscillator Press thanks the following corporate sponsors for helping to make this project a success:

The Rose & Crown serves traditional English fare with new world flair. The family friendly restaurant, separate pub, and scenic patio offers something for everyone right at the beginning of Main Street in Canmore.

Phone: 403.678.5168
Location:
        749 Railway Ave.
        Canmore, AB

Anderwerks Motorrad Spezialist is Canada's largest independent BMW service, repair, restoration, and performance tuning facility.

Web: Anderwerks.com
Phone: 403.277.4269
GPS: N 51' 05.184' W 114'02.889'
Location:
        #4,3704-6th St NE
        Calgary, Alberta

The Ted Simon Foundation encourages adventure travellers to illuminate what's going on in the world beyond the generalizations of the media, to go the extra mile and to share their honest experiences through writing, film and photography.

Web: JupitersTravellers.org
Email: explore@jupiterstravellers.org
Loaction:
         California, USA

Special thanks to:

Alice Kroeker

John Colyer